- Your Free Gift
- I wanted to show my appreciation
- I've put together a free gift for you.

EASY BONE BROTH: TOP 45 Recipes For Instant Weight Loss And Powerful Health Improvement.

http://www.iqtravels.com/gift-easy-bone-broth

- Just visit the link above to download it now.
  - I know you will love this gift.
    - Thanks!
    - Richard Leroy

Table of Contents

Introduction — 4

Chapter 1: The Basic Fundamentals of Air Fryer Cooking — 6
- Know Your Air Fryer — 6
- The Structure of Your Air Fryer — 7
- The Core Features of Your Air Fryer — 11
- The Basic Preparation and using procedure of your Air Fryer — 12
- Some Common Mistakes To Avoid — 17

Chapter 2: Breakfast Recipes — 20
- Air Fried French toast Sticks — 20
- Air Fried Cranberry Muffins — 24
- Cheese And Mushroom Frittata — 27
- Bacon and Cheese Rolls — 30
- Croissant With Ham, Mushroom, and Egg — 33

Chapter 3: Lunch Recipes — 36
- Mac And Cheese — 36
- Jerk Style Chicken Wings — 39
- Baked Heirloom Tomatoes With Feta Pesto — 42
- Roasted Rack Of Lamb with A Macadamia Crust — 45
- Teriyaki Glazed Halibut Steak — 48

Chapter 4: Dinner Recipes — 51
- Meat Balls and Creamy Potatoes — 51
- Crab Cakes — 55
- Air Fried Spring Rolls — 58
- Fish Nuggets — 61
- Breaded Fish Fillets — 64

Chapter 5: Desert Recipes — 67
- Chocolate Cake — 67
- Apricot Blackberry Crumble — 70

Vanilla Soufflé	73
Soft Chocolate Brownies With Caramel Sauce	76
Mini Apple Pie	79

Chapter 6 : Vegetables Recipes — 82

Paneer and Cheese Balls	82
Samosa	85
Vegetable Spring Rolls	88
Semolina Cutlets	92
Onion Pakora	95

Chapter 7 : High Protein Recipes — 98

Chimichurri Skirt Steak	98
Salmon With Dill Sauce	101
Cajun Shrimp	104
Paprika Roast Chicken With Crispy Potato Rosti	107
Roast Potatoes With Bacon and Garlic	110

Chapter 8: Few More Interesting Bonus Recipes! — 112

Panko Crusted Fish Fillet With Chips	112
Panko Crusted Fish Fillet With Chips	117
Vegetable Crisps and Cheesy Pesto Twist	122
Thai Roast Beef Salad With Nam Jim Dressing	126
Salmon With Creamy Courgette	130

Conclusion — 134

Introduction

Food is something without which the human race will so go into extinction and ever since the conception of the human race, they have been constantly seeking new ways to make their meals as delicious and savory as possible. Just have a look at the Neanderthals who started their culinary journey by simply feasting upon the raw meat of hunted animals, and then eventually evolved themselves into using fire to cook those meats which soon became the staple method for food preparation. Thanks to our ancestors, the knowledge of being able to cook food with fire has been passed down to use throughout generations after generations.

Evolution has now brought us to an age where humankind now aims not only to eat any kind of food which they want, but they have grown the tendency to eat healthy alternative to oily and heavy foods which would retain the flavor while at the same time minimize the negative effects that might be accompanied by them.

The solution to this problem eventually came through the marriage of modern culinary methodologies and advanced technologies which gave us better and more efficient products to expand up a completely new dimension for cooking food bestowing upon us kitchen appliances like the Microwave Oven, Electric Grill, Toaster Machine and now the device that has been creating whirlwind amongst cuisine aficionados the Air Fryer!

Since the technology of the Air Fryer is still relatively new, there are people who are still roaming around in a void helplessly without any knowledge of what to do after buying this magnificent device! This particular book is targeted towards both absolute new comers and professional Air Fryer users who are looking to push the potential of their device to its fullest extent.

The structure which has been implemented in this book will allow you to deeply understand the nooks and crannies' of your Air Fryer and learn how you will be able to craft mouthwatering dishes which you never thought was possible!

We all know that fast foods are extremely delicious and it's really hard to get past McDonalds without grabbing a bag of French Fries! But we are also aware of the cholesterol values that come with them as baggage and damage our heart to an even greater extent.

With Air Fryer now in your hands, those days will be soon long gone as you will be able to enjoy all of your favorite foods that you have been craving for without instilling the fear of gaining too much of weight or causing much damage to your body.

This book will help you unlock the secrets of your Air Fryer through which you finally will be able to enjoy all of the unhealthy foods out there, in a surprisingly healthy way!

I want to take a moment and appreciate your generous gesture for purchasing this book, and now I would like you to stay with me and begin your journey into the world of Air Fryer Cooking.

Be prepared to make everything from French Fries to Chicken Wings to even muffins with the usage of minimal oil while still retaining that appetizing texture and palatable flavor!

Chapter 1: The Basic Fundamentals of Air Fryer Cooking

At this moment I am assuming that you are completely new to the Air Fryer scene and would like to know more about the appliance which you have purchased or would like to purchase. So, just like any proper guidebook, let me first walk you through what exactly an Air Fryer is and what makes it so revolutionary.

Know Your Air Fryer

The most fundamental thing which you should know about it is special mode of cooking that differentiates it from the rest of the crowd. While other Kitchen Appliance usually relies mostly on conduction heating, the Air Fryer takes advantage of the convection heating system and the very essence of our life, "The Air" to prepared and cooks the dishes which we want it to. Back when it was first created, this technology was absolutely groundbreaking which led to the ascension of many eyebrows of amateur cooks and chefs alike.

After the intake chamber of the Air Fryer has sucked up the air, the appliance superheats it to about 200°C and passes it to a very specialized heating chamber where the food is cooked. You might've noticed that many Air Fryers bear with them the words "Rapid Air Technology", the process which I just mentioned earlier is exactly what they refer to as being the Rapid Air Technology.

The use of extremely hot air eliminates the requirement of using a heavy amount of oil and gives you the flexibility to create your favorite dish through frying, grilling, baking and even roasting without ultimately leaving your dishes floating in a barrage of oil.

The Structure of Your Air Fryer

Before a doctor goes on to operate on a human body, he always first begins by fully understanding observing the various parts and mechanisms of the human body in order to be able to perform his surgeries properly with grace and mitigating the chances of errors. The basic thing to learn from here is that before planning on starting to thoroughly use a device, it is essential for you to know what are the different parts and mechanism that makes up the appliance as a whole. Having a better understanding will simply help you to utilize the device with greater efficiency. Keeping that in mind, here I will be showing you the basic body parts which an Air Fryer is typically comprised of.

- **The Cooking Chamber:** This is the place where the magic happens and the food actually gets cooked. The functionality here varies a little bit depending on which branded Fryer you are using in the sense that the cooking chamber might come with the capacity of holding just a single tray or a multi-layered tray.

- **Heating Element:** The heating element is responsible for the level of heat which needs to be transferred to the passing Air. A Very desirable feature amongst most Air Fryer is that whenever it reaches the specified temperature for cooking, the heating elements automatically turns itself off as to save power and prevent further overheating.

- **Fan and Grill:** The fan and the grill tend to work in conjunction with each other in order to ensure that superheated air is evenly distributed around your food. The mechanical design of the grill allows it to adjust the direction of the air flow giving which plays a large part in the whole cooking process.

- **Exhaust System:** The exhaust system in this appliance is device is designed to help maintain a stable internal pressure and prevent build up harmful air. Some models go to another extent in adding a filter which clears out the dust and other leftover particles to clean out the exhausted air making sure that it does not release any unpleasant odor.

- **Transferable Food Tray:** This is basically the tray where you are going to place the food which you want to be cooked. There are some brands out there which gives you the added advantage of having several boundary walls built within the tray itself to allow you cook dishes of several different types at once. Other than that, some brands might even provide a universal handle using which you will be able to pull out your tray from the heating chamber with ease.

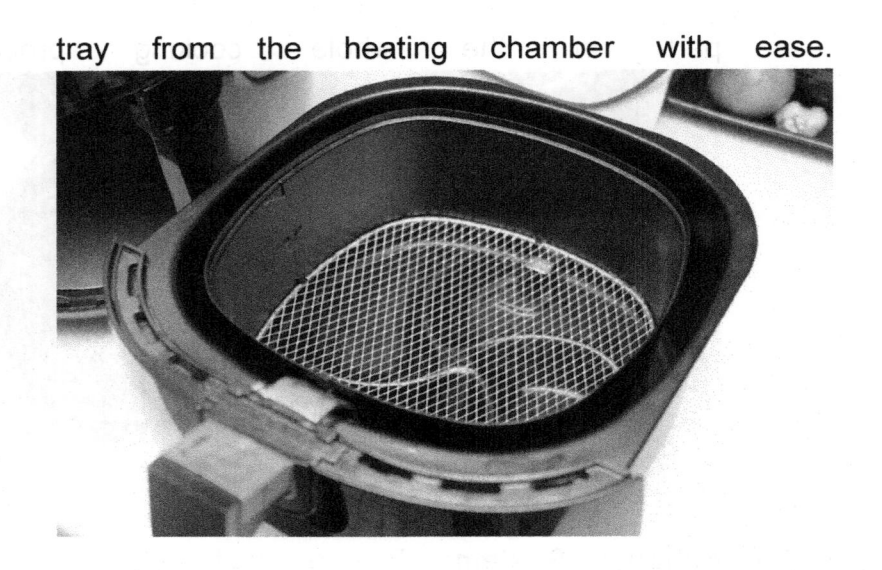

The Core Features of Your Air Fryer

While different brands usually tend to offer something of an extra to make sure that their Air Fryer has something more for the users, some of the features of an Air Fryer are almost regarded as being a staple to all available models.

- **Automatic Temperature Control Mechanism:** This is perhaps one of the most important and prominent features of the device which detects the level of temperature of airflow and stops the heating whenever your desired temperature is achieved. This allows the appliance to ensure that the dishes are always cooked to fulfill the desires of the chef.
- **Fully Digitized Screen and Touch Mechanism:** The manufacturers of the Air Fryers always keeps in mind that some of their consumers might be master of the culinary arts or expert chefs. This feature is added for

those particular individuals giving them a greater level of accessibility and allowing them to cook with just a few simple taps.
- **Buzzer and Timer Feature:** Sometimes simply staring at the appliance until the food is cooked to perfection might get a little boring and so the buzzer system in implement here to give you a sense of freedom while your Air Fryer is cooking your meal. It allows you to set a kind of an alarm to let you know via audio cues when the timer runs out and it's time for you to take out the food.
- **Cooking Presets:** These are fixed temperature settings that have been pre-installed in the Air-Fryer that lets you cook with no-effort and with just a simple touch. The Pre-sets are given for various meals and dishes saving you from the hassle of having to remember the settings for every single basic dish out there.

The Basic Preparation and using procedure of your Air Fryer

Your quest for creating healthy and delicious food is not far away not is difficult at all using the Air Fryer since it has been meticulously designed keeping in mind the full accessibility of its users. The very basic outline for the cooking most dishes follows these simple steps:

- At first, bring out the transferrable tray from the cooking chamber and drizzle it with just a small amount of oil.
- Take all the ingredients of your food or the whole food if you wish, and put them in the drizzled tray.

- Depending on the food which you are cooking, set your cooking temperature and the time.
- This step is not required for every food, but most wait will require you to shake the food basket half way through the cooking.
- Finally, just wait for the timer to end and voila! Food is ready.

Since only a very minimal amount of oil is used in contrast to the more oil drenched procedures, it instantly cuts down the fat value of the food by 80% which is an expansive jump, considering that similar foods are going to be consumed every day.

Below is a small list of the most common food items which you might be interested in trying out during your first ventures, alongside their most basic preparation instructions.

- **Thick Frozen Fries**

    Min Amount: 11oz.
    Maximum Amount: 43oz
    Time Taken: 12 – 22 minutes
    Temperature: 360 °F
    Halfway Shake Need: Yes
    Extra Remarks: Nil

- **Thin Frozen Fries**

    Min Amount: 11oz.
    Maximum Amount: 43oz.
    Time Taken: 9 – 19 minutes
    Temperature: 360 °F
    Halfway Shake Need: Yes
    Extra Remarks: Nil

- **Homemade Fries**

    Min Amount: 11oz. / 21oz.
    Maximum Amount: 32oz. /43oz.
    Time Taken: 15 – 22 minutes / 18 – 25 minutes
    Temperature: 360 °F
    Halfway Shake Need: Yes
    Extra Remarks: You will need to soak fries for 30 minutes in ¼ tablespoon of oil for 11oz.; 3/4rth tablespoon for 32oz.; ½ tablespoon for 21oz. and 1 tablespoon for 43oz.

- **Potato Wedges**

    Min Amount: 11oz. / 21oz.
    Maximum Amount: 32oz.
    Time Taken: 18 – 21 minutes / 24 minutes
    Temperature: 360 °F
    Halfway Shake Need: Yes
    Extra Remarks: You will need to soak fries for 30 minutes in ¼ tablespoon of oil for 11oz.; 3/4rth tablespoon for 32oz.; ½ tablespoon for 21oz.

- **Potato Cubes**

    Min Amount: 11oz. / 21oz.
    Maximum Amount: 32oz.
    Time Taken: 18 – 21 minutes / 24 minutes
    Temperature: 360 °F
    Halfway Shake Need: Yes
    Extra Remarks: You will need to soak fries for 30 minutes in ¼ tablespoon of oil for 11oz.; 3/4rth tablespoon for 32oz.; ½ tablespoon for 21oz.

- **Cheese Sticks**

    Min Amount: 4oz.
    Maximum Amount: 16oz.
    Time Taken: 8 - 10 minutes
    Temperature: 360 °F
    Halfway Shake Need: Yes
    Extra Remarks: Nil

- **Cheese Sticks**

    Min Amount: 11oz.
    Maximum Amount: 43oz.
    Time Taken: 9 – 19 minutes
    Temperature: 360 °F
    Halfway Shake Need: Yes
    Extra Remarks: Preferable to use Oven Ready Version.

- **Chicken Nuggets**

    Min Amount: 1oz.
    Maximum Amount: 14.
    Time Taken: 6 minutes
    Temperature: 330/390 °F
    Halfway Shake Need: Yes
    Extra Remarks: Preferable to use Oven Ready version.

- **Fish Sticks**

    Min Amount: 4oz.
    Maximum Amount: 12oz.

Time Taken: 8 – 10 minutes
Temperature: 390 °F
Halfway Shake Need: No
Extra Remarks: Preferably use oven ready version.

- **Steak**

  Min Amount: 4oz.
  Maximum Amount: 21oz.
  Time Taken: 5 min 360°F – 4 min 150°F / 6 min 360°F – 4 min 150°F
  Temperature: 360 °F
  Halfway Shake Need: No
  Extra Remarks: Nil

- **Hamburger**

  Min Amount: 4oz.
  Maximum Amount: 14oz.
  Time Taken: 6/7 minutes
  Temperature: 360 °F
  Halfway Shake Need: No
  Extra Remarks: Nil

- **Chicken Wings**

  Min Amount: 3oz.
  Maximum Amount: 21oz.
  Time Taken: 18 to 22 minutes
  Temperature: 360 °F
  Halfway Shake Need: No
  Extra Remarks: Nil

- **Chicken Breast**

  Min Amount: 3oz.
  Maximum Amount: 21oz.
  Time Taken: 8min 390°F – 10 min 360°F / 8 min 290°F – 8 min 360°F
  Temperature: 360 °F
  Halfway Shake Need: No
  Extra Remarks: Nil

- **Cake**

  Min Amount: 1oz.
  Maximum Amount: 24oz.
  Time Taken: 30 minutes
  Temperature: 320 °F
  Halfway Shake Need: No
  Extra Remarks: Nil

Some Common Mistakes To Avoid

Whenever there is a new device which is ripe to be explored, it is always mostly accompanied with some very common mistakes which are made by its first-time users. The Air Fryer is no exception and its users also have their fair share of mistakes which they sometimes make. It is better to know about these mistakes earlier and be prepared for the complications which one might face during their early life.

- Always bear in mind that you are not supposed to heat up your fryer prior to using it. Pre-heating is not required and not recommended with this appliance. It is a common habit for people who have the tendency to pre-heat their oven or grill before baking or grilling anything. But doing this with the Air Fryer will only result in an imperfect dish with uneven cooking. So, what you should do just before starting to fry, you can start the Air Fryer and let it heat up for just 2 minutes and then put your food inside the cooking chamber.

- Some housewives hold the misconception that using the black tray of any toaster will help you to bake better since it absorbs more heat, but this is dead wrong, and this CAN lead your Air Fryer to become unusable, not to mention ruin your perfectly prepared food! When you are using a black tray, the destruction of your baked goods won't depend on your set temperature at all. Instead, thanks to the tray's better heat absorbing capacity, the lower of part of our cake will quickly turn black while the upper surface will remain raw, leaving behind a very charred piece of bakery. Therefore, it is highly recommended that you use a tray that resembles a little lighter color for baking.
- In some cases, it is quite normal to ignore the instructions distilled for selecting the appropriate frying or baking mode since they don't bring about a major change in the heating method of the appliance, but the scenario in terms of the Air Fryer is largely different. It is very essential here to choose the proper frying method as it directly impacts on which of the heaters are in the Air Fryer is going to be active (Top and Bottom). So for example, if you chose a grill option for only one sided grill, then the bottom heater might only be turned on, alternatively if you choose a double sided grill then both the top and bottom heaters will be used. This should be kept in mind even more if you intend to do baking. But you have to keep in mind that regardless of the type of frying mode you choose, you

will still need to pay close attention to the selected temperature for your cooking your dish.
- A general concern when cooking frozen foods is that should oil be added to it while cooking. Well, the simple answer to this is that no, adding oil is not necessary when cooking frozen fries and they turn out to be just as crispy. But it's essential to soak then under water for about an hour and then drizzle just a small amount of oil to the Air Fryer before cooking.

Chapter 2: Breakfast Recipes

Air Fried French toast Sticks

French toast is perhaps one the oldest known and existing product known to mankind to resemble the likings of a proper English breakfast. The roots of French Toast goes back all the way to the ancient era of 14th century German where it was first recorded to be discovered by men, and thus it was dubbed as being "German Toast". Later on, the recipe has travelled through time and across multiple generations holding names such as Gypsy Toast or Poor Knights! Until finally, it reached the golden age of the 21st century where now it has become an inseparable part of any English and/or American man's breakfast! Using Air Fryer, it is possible to create French Toasts with absolute ease, and they can also be broken down into small stick sizes to make them more attractive to children! Yummy.

Portion

This particular recipe will help you create French toast for 2 servings.

Total Time

This recipe will take about 17 minutes to make.

Ingredients

- 4 slices of bread (Any kind, depending on your preference)
- Approximately 2 tablespoons of soft butter/ as an alternative margarine can be used to butter the breads.
- 2 gently beaten eggs
- Salt as required
- Cinnamon as required
- Nutmeg as required
- Ground Clove spices as required
- For purpose of garnishing, you can go for Icing sugar or the much more lavish and delicious maple syrup!

Nutritional Values

- Calories : 384
- Fat : 18g
- Saturated Fat : 4g
- Carbohydrates : 41g
- Protein : 6g
- Dietary Fiber : 1.4g
- Cholesterol : 0g

How to Make The Dish

- The very first step which you will need to follow here to prepare your Air Fryer for the task at hand by pre-heating it to a level of 180°C
- While your Air Fryer is being warmed up, go ahead and take a bowl. Crack two eggs and pour them in, add just a pinch of salt with a few aggressive shakes of cinnamon from your grinder and pinches of nutmeg along with ground cloves to give your toast a fine basic flavor.
- Keep that bowl away, and tend to your breads now. Butter them up properly on both sides using perhaps a buttering brush and cut them into individual strips of identical sizes. Please note that it is not strictly necessary that you are only allowed to go for strips, you can if you want, cut them up in star shapes as well!
- Once you have set everything in motion, then gently drizzle up the bread pieces by soaking them up properly under the bread beaten egg, and finely arrange them in a fashionable line inside your Air Fryer.
- The total cooking time for this dish will be 6 minutes. 2 minutes required for each side. So once you have put your bread slices inside the fryer, wait for 2 minutes until one side has reached a gorgeous golden brown complexion. Bring out the tray and spray a generous amount of cooking spray on top of the breads.
- Once sprayed, flip them up and repeat the same process again but this time, let it cook for 4 minutes more.
- Wait until the breads are all evenly cooked and then let your taste buds dance!

Air Fried Cranberry Muffins

Cranberry Muffins has long been an ideal part of the English tradition. These pieces are not healthy jam packed with health benefits that arrive from the usage of Cranberries, but are also supremely delicious to the point of being devilish! These Muffins are low in fat and cholesterol but high in health values, making them a very suitable food to start your engines in the morning!

Portion

This particular recipe will help you create about 12 pieces of Cranberry Muffins.

Total Time

This recipe will take about 17 minutes to make.

Ingredients

- 1/3 cups of softened and salted butter which are cut into cubes

- ½ cup of granulated sugar
- 1 piece of medium sized egg
- About 180ml of pasteurized pure milk
- ½ tablespoons of vanilla essence
- About 1 and a quarter cup of plain everyday flour that is properly and thoroughly sifted.
- ½ teaspoon of baking powder sifted alongside the flour.
- ½ teaspoon of baking soda also sifted alongside the flour.
- About 75 grams of dried cranberries, or more if you wish depending on your flavor palate.
- Walnuts as required
- Cashews as required
- Almonds as required

Nutritional Values (Per Piece)

- Calories : 172
- Fat : 4g
- Saturated Fat : 1g
- Carbohydrates : 24g
- Protein : 5g
- Dietary Fiber : 0g
- Cholesterol : 36mg

How to Make The Dish

- The very first step of this dish is taking your time and let your Air Fryer pre-heat up to about a temperature of 180 degree Celsius.
- Use an electric mixer if possible and beat the butter, mixing it up with the sugar until it is absolutely fluffy and a little bit pale. It is possible to do this by hand as well, but it will be very tiresome and time-consuming.

- Crack the egg into a mixer, and gently beat it up for a few minutes. After that, add up your vanilla essence to the egg and taking turns, mix up your milk and flour until none of the ingredients remain.
- Beat again with everything mixed in for about 2-3 minutes until it gains a good consistency and it feels like everything is properly mixed up.
- Once the batter is ready and smooth according to your desires, switch off your electric mixer, take spoon or spatula and add in the dried cranberries along with the nuts.
- Pour the batter into the Cupcake liners until they are full and dreamy and bake them at a temperature of 160 degree Celsius for 15 minutes. (Since you are going for an Air Fryer, it is highly recommended that you use large cupcake containers with a thick paper which are much stronger than the regular ones.)
- Bring them out once they are done, let them cool and start drooling over them! They are yours for the taking!

Cheese And Mushroom Frittata

In Italy, the word "Frittata" holds a very deep value in the sense that it refers to an overly healthy and delicious alternative to Omelets' or Egg poaches. Speaking in the most general term, the word Frittata has been derived from the word "Friggere" which roughly translates to "fried". Until the late 1950s, most of the world used the word Frittata to simply denote an omelet, but that has drastically changed as nowadays Frittata directly points towards the delicious crustless cuisine which is an elder brother of the Omelette mixed up with cheese, vegetables and/or pasta!

Portion

This particular recipe will help you create about servings for 4 people.

Total Time

This recipe will take about 30-40 minutes to make.

Ingredients

- 1/3 cups of softened and salted butter which are cut into cubes
- ½ cup of granulated sugar
- 1 piece of medium sized egg
- 1 whole piece of Red Onion
- About 2 tablespoons of Olive Oil
- About 4 cups of fine button Mushrooms
- 6 pieces of medium sized eggs.
- Salt as required
- 6 tables spoon of feta cheese, preferably crumbled.

Nutritional Values (Per Piece)

- Calories : 172
- Fat : 4g
- Saturated Fat : 1g
- Carbohydrates : 24g
- Protein : 5g
- Dietary Fiber : 0g
- Cholesterol : 36mg

How to Make The Dish

- o This dish will require you to first individually create the onion and mushroom sauté to be used later on with your actual dish.
- o To create your Onion and mushroom sauté, you will need to peel of your onions (making sure that you don't start crying) and slice them down into ¼ inch round thin portions.
- o Wash the button mushroom on a separate side and treat the same way as your onions cutting them in thin rounds as well.

- Take the two ingredients into a pan, heating it up over a very gentle medium flame until both of them have sweated enough to obtain a tender texture.
- Once you think that they are done, pull them up and transfer the sauté mixture onto a dry kitchen towel to let it drain and cool down.
- Since the sauté is no ready, you can turn your head towards the Air Fryer now, start it up by preheating it to 165 degree Celsius.
- Take a separate bowl and crack all of the 6 eggs into that bowl and start whisking it gently with your desired amount of salt. Start with gentle beatings with aggressive ones later.
- Take an 8-inch baking dish and apply a very thin layer of pan spray on top of making sure that the internal parts, as well as the bottom parts, are fully coated.
- Take the bowl with you beaten egg, and pour them down into the pan along with your onion and mushroom sauté. Top it off with the crumbled cheeslings which I assume you had kept separated.
- Take the filled baking tray and place it inside the Air Fryers cooking chamber and let it sit there.
- It should take about 30 minutes for the dish to be cooked, after it is done, bring it out and serve!

Pro Tip: If you are confused about whether or not your dish is done, you can check it by sticking it up with a knife through the middle and see if anything comes up. If the knife comes out clean, then your dish is done!

Bacon and Cheese Rolls

We all know that bakers Delight has been the pioneer when it comes to making delicious bread rolls using yeast to fluff them up and turn them into mouthwatering creations of heaven. Their stuff rolls full which are full of cheese are to die for, and it's a dream for people to be able to replicate that same flavor. Well, good news for you is that now you apparently can! And you can even make 10 times more delicious because here, along with your cheese stuffing, you are also adding up an exquisite layer of bacon topping!

Portion

This particular recipe will help you create about servings for 4 people.

Total Time

This recipe will take about 15-20 minutes to make.

Ingredients

- 1 big block of extremely sharp grated cheddar cheese
- 1 pound of chopped bacon, carefully kept at room temperature
- About 8 ounces of crescent rolls which should measure up to a single can.

Nutritional Values (Per Piece)

- Calories : 291
- Fat : 9g
- Saturated Fat : 5g
- Carbohydrates : 30g
- Protein : 12g
- Dietary Fiber : 0g
- Cholesterol : 0mg

How to Make The Dish

- The perfection of this dish relies a lot upon the level of attention you give to the scale of preparation behind each the initial creation process of this baked good, with that in mind, start up this recipe by firing up your Ari Fryer to a pre-heated temperature of 330 degree Fahrenheit or 165 degree Celsius.
- Take some time to gently caress the crescent roll dough and measure about 1 inch by 1.5 inch pieces, and cut them out using a sharp knife.
- Take the grated cheese which presumably you kept earlier on the side and mix It up with the bacon. After which, measure up just about quarter a cup of the cheese and bacon mixture, pick it up and transfer it to the middle part of each dough sheet.

- Take special care here, because you are going to close up the dough sheets now, ensuring that the mixture does not overflow and come out from the top like erupting lava.
- The final part of the dish will require you to pick up the gentle rolls which are now packed with bacon and cheese and throw them in, into the Air Fray tray or Food basket, which ever you might prefer to choose.
- At the specified temperature of 390 Degrees Fahrenheit, for the baking to be completely done, it should take somewhere around six to eight minutes.

Pro Tip: The time cannot be told with strict accuracy since various factors are coming into play here, but the best way to know if your goods are ready is to keep your eye peeled and look out for the appearing of a smooth golden brown texture, letting you know that they are ready to be eaten and devoured by you!

Croissant With Ham, Mushroom, and Egg

Always staying at home and eating the same kind of food over and over again, might actually make your mind wander around outsides sometimes to seek foods which are healthy yet at the same time partially exotic to eat. Sometimes you might just happen to stumble upon one of those café's which serves some of the most delicious Croissant coupled up with Ham and Eggs, which makes your taste buds jingle the happy song. If you are one such person, and you are looking to add a little adventure to your morning breakfast, then fear no more as this recipe has got you fully covered and will help you create you very own cafe styled breakfast!

Portion

This particular recipe will help you create about servings for 1 person (1 piece)

Total Time

This recipe will take about 13 minutes to make. 5 minutes dedicated to preparation and 8 minutes dedicated for cooking.

Ingredients

- 1 Croissant, preferably bought from the store.
- About 3 slices of finely Honey shaved Ham
- 4 Quartered pieces of small button mushroom
- 3 Halved pieces of Honey Cherry Tomato
- About 50g of Shredded Cheddar or Mozzarella Cheese
- 1 piece of large egg
- About ½ a sprig of Rosemary that needs to roughly chopped
- About a handful of Salad Greens.

Nutritional Values (Per Piece)

- Calories : 410
- Fat : 22g
- Saturated Fat : 12g
- Carbohydrates : 35g
- Protein : 18g
- Dietary Fiber : 1g
- Cholesterol : 50mg

How to Make The Dish

- Similar to all manners of baking, this dish is also going to ask you to pre heat your Air Fryer to about 160 degree Celsius.
- The first thing which you will have to do for this dish is to get a baking dish of dimension 16x10x4 cm and grease it up with ample amount of butter to make sure

- that the ingredients don't stay sticking to the side of the dish after baking is complete.
- Perfectly align and arrange all of the ingredients in two separate layers, making sure that the shredded cheese is at the middle and upper layer of the dish.
- There should be some space in the middle of the ham mixture, if there is not, make some space and crack the egg and pour it in.
- Sprinkle in some of the freshly grounded black pepper and add just a pinch of salt with rosemary spread all around the mixture.
- Place it in the frying pan, alongside the Croissant in the Air Fryer and let bake inside it for about 8 minutes.
- The total time is 8 minutes, but you should be aware because you will have to remove the croissant from the basket after the 4 minutes mark.
- Finally, take a serving plate and arrange everything according to your heart's desire! Place the croissant on one side and the cheesy baked egg on the other alongside with the green salads and start eating it up immediately!

Chapter 3: Lunch Recipes

Mac And Cheese

What can I say more about Macaroni and Cheese that you don't know already! This is perhaps one of the most staple pasta-esque meals known to teenagers when it comes to American English dishes. Mac and Cheese has been filling up the tummies of people all around the world in their lunch and it does it for good reason! The seamless incorporation of ingredients such as breadcrumbs, vegetables and even meat if you want! Makes this one of the easiest to make yet versatile luncheon item to date!

Portion

This particular recipe will help you create about servings for 1 person (1 piece)

Total Time

This recipe will take about 20 minutes.

Ingredients

- About a cup of Elbow shaped Macaroni
- About ½ cup of Broccoli/ Cauliflower
- About ½ cup of warmed Milk
- About 1 and a half cup of grated Cheddar Cheese.
- Salt as required
- Pepper as required
- About 1 tablespoon of grated Parmesan Cheese.

Nutritional Values (Per 100gm)

- Calories : 164
- Fat : 5g
- Saturated Fat : 1.6g
- Carbohydrates : 23
- Protein : 7g
- Dietary Fiber : 1.2g
- Cholesterol : 8mg

How to Make The Dish

- Excited to make your very own Mac and Cheese? Well, chill out and follow these simple steps to have your dreams come true! But first, start everything by pre-heating your Air Fryer to about 200 Degree Celsius.
- After that, the time comes to boil up the Macaroni, so for this step what you will want to do is bring a pot of water to a hot boil and add your macaroni's alongside the vegetables, bearing in mind that the temperature

here is needed to be trimmed down a little bit to the medium side.
- Keep on simmering until your macaroni seems to be perfect and the vegetable appear to be tender but not too much soft and mushy.

    Pro Tip: An almost perfect timing for this is about 7-10 minutes.

- After which, take some time to drain out the water from the pasta and veggies and return to them their homely pot.
- Take your time to add some generous proportions of Cheddar Cheese to the Macaroni and vegetables, since they are already warm, you can simply toss the cheese in which will cause them to melt and get mixed.
- Season the mixture with some salt and pepper as desired.
- Pour the whole of the pasta over and ovenproof dish and sprinkle the parmesan cheese all over it.
- Adjust the temperature of your Air Fryer to 1180 degree Celsius and carefully put the tray with the Pasta in it, inside the cooking chamber of your Air Fryer and let it bake there about 15 minutes.
- Before serving, try to hold yourself down and let it cool down for 10 minutes, otherwise, you might burn your tongue!

    Pro Tip: A very easy way to detect if your Pasta is properly done is by keeping an eye for the moment when you Pasta will start to bubble.

Jerk Style Chicken Wings

The normal flavors and spices aren't just cutting it out anymore for you aren't they? You are looking to dive into the territories of the extremists and conjure up yourself something spicy enough to turn you into a fire-breathing dragon? The Jamaican jerk Style Chicken Wings is just what you are looking for! Completely drizzled with the eye-watering Jamaican Jerk Spice, these chicken wings are prepared through the Jamaican technique of jerking which involves total marinating of the wings by rubbing them with the said spices. If this does not turn on your fiery grill, then I don't know what will!

Portion

This particular recipe will help you create about servings for 5 persons.

Total Time

This recipe will take about 30 minutes of your cooking time while around 2 hours or so will be needed for preparation.

Ingredients

- 3 pound of chicken wings
- About 2 tablespoons of Olive Oil
- About 2 tablespoons of Soy Sauce
- About 6 cloves of finely chopped garlic.
- Habanero Peppers (It is essential to thoroughly remove the seeds and rinds before chopping them up)
- Allspice as required
- Cinnamon as required
- Cayenne Pepper as required
- White pepper as required
- Salt as required
- 2 tablespoon of Brown Sugar
- A tablespoon of finely chopped fresh thyme
- A tablespoon of finely grated ginger
- About 4 scallions
- About 5 tablespoons of lime juice
- About ½ a cup of red wine vinegar

Nutritional Values (Per Piece)

- Calories : 160
- Fat : 10g
- Saturated Fat : 2.5g
- Carbohydrates : 3g
- Protein : 15g
- Dietary Fiber : 1g
- Cholesterol : 90mg

How to Make The Dish

  o The very first thing which you are going to have to do, is prepare the marinade for this dish, and how are you

going to that? Well, mix everything except on the list except the chicken in a bowl!
- After your marinade is complete, take the chicken wing pieces and gently place them down in the marinade, ensuring carefully that all of the pieces are properly showered and drenched with the mixture.
- Take the mixture and place it inside a container or a resalable bag and place it inside a refrigerator. The marinating of the chicken will continue for up to at least 2 hours before you are to take out.
- Just before taking out the Marinated chicken, you will want to take a little bit of time and preheat the temperature of your Air Fryer to about 390 degrees Fahrenheit or 198 Degree Celsius.
- Take out the chicken wing pieces from the marinade, and drain them out by patting them against paper towels.
- Gently place the chicken in the cooking tray and place it inside the cooking chamber. Let it cook for about 10 minutes.
- After 10 minutes, take out the food tray from the cooking chamber and give it a little shake, and then let it cook for 10 minutes.
- After which, the only thing left for you to do will be to slowly bring out the tray, serve the chickens and unleash your wild side!

Baked Heirloom Tomatoes With Feta Pesto

The mixture of Heirloom tomatoes and Feta cheese has been a classical county favorite for years now. If you are in the mode for something a little bit off beat, then you should definitely add this to your next lunch menu! This little dish will throw you back into the good old days where genuine farmed products were still cool!

Portion

This particular recipe will help you create about servings for 4 persons.

Total Time

This recipe will take about 20-25 minutes of your cooking time.

Ingredients

Pesto:

- Roughly half a cup of chopped parsley and basil.
- About half a cup of grated parmesan cheese
- 3 tablespoon of toasted pine nuts
- 1 toasted clove of garlic
- Just a pinch of salt

Tomatoes and Feta:

- At least 2 heirloom Tomatoes
- A block of 8 ounce Feta Cheese
- ½ cup of paper thing round slices of red onion
- A tablespoon of olive oil
- Just a pinch of salt

Nutritional Values

- Calories : 316
- Fat : 15.1g
- Saturated Fat : 8g
- Carbohydrates : 30.7g
- Protein : 14.7g

How to Make The Dish

- o The first thing which you will need to do for this particular dish is to prepare the Pesto itself properly, this is a very crucial ingredient here and you will need to follow the steps by word. So, first off, combine every single ingredient that is listed above for the pesto by tossing them into a food processor.

- Next, while the processor is still running, gently add the olive oil in such a way that it runs down into a thin stream until all of the oil is fully incorporated with the Pesta.
- Keep it refrigerated until it is required again.
- After that, go ahead and pre-heat your air Fryer to 390 degrees Fahrenheit, which stands at about 198 degree Celsius,
- Take the tomatoes and feta cheese; slice them down to ½ inch thick slices.
- Drizzle down the olive oil into the red onion slices and toss them in, furthermore, top off the tomato and feta slices with red onions.
- Gently arrange the organized tomato and feta slices into the food tray and cook them inside the air fryer for about 12-14 minutes. The way you are going to measure if your food is cooked is by looking at the color texture of the feta which should, in the end, give a soft and brown complexion.
- Finally, toss in just a pinch of salt and situate a dollop of pesto on the top of each individual piece.

Roasted Rack Of Lamb with A Macadamia Crust

Nothing can beat the majestic nature of the lamb rack. Just having this magnificent dish at your lunch table is going to enhance the whole value of the table by ten folds! Lose yourself with this finely crafted dish that incorporates the juicy tenderness of lamb rack meats along with the crunchiness bestowed upon from the Macadamia nuts, perfect for big parties or family outings.

Portion

This particular recipe will help you create about servings for 4-6 persons.

Total Time

This recipe will take about 10 minutes of your cooking time, but with the preparation timing, it will take about 40 minutes in total.

Ingredients

- 1 piece of garlic clove
- About 1 table spoon of olive oil
- 1 and ¾rth pound of lamb rack
- Pepper as required
- Salt as required

Macadamia Crust:

- 3 ounces of pure macadamia nuts (unsalted)
- About 1 tablespoon of breadcrumbs
- About 1 tablespoon of freshly chopped rosemary
- 1 piece of egg

Nutritional Values

- Calories : 507
- Fat : 43g
- Saturated Fat : 13g
- Carbohydrates : 2g
- Protein : 27g
- Cholesterol: 136mg

How to Make The Dish

- The first step for this dish is to finely chop up the garlic and mix them up with the olive oil to make a garlic oil mixture.
- Using the mixture, gently brush over the rack of the lamb and sprinkle some pepper and salt for seasoning.
- Chop up the nuts and place gently put them into a bowl, toss in the breadcrumbs alongside rosemary's.

- Crack the egg into another bowl and whisk it properly the mix it in with the former mixture.
- Next, to do the actual coating of the lamb, you are going to have to dip the meat into the egg mixture, drain off the excess and coat the lamb using the macadamia crust.
- The final step here is to put the coated lamb rack inside the tray and place it inside the cooking chamber.
- A very important thing to keep in mind here is the timing, first off you are going to need to set the timer to 30 minutes after that has passed you are will have to increase the temperature to 390 degrees Fahrenheit and then set the timer for an extra 5 minutes. When the five minutes will be over, you are going to remove the meat and leave the rest there, covering it with a tin foil before giving it to the guests for them to swallow!

Teriyaki Glazed Halibut Steak

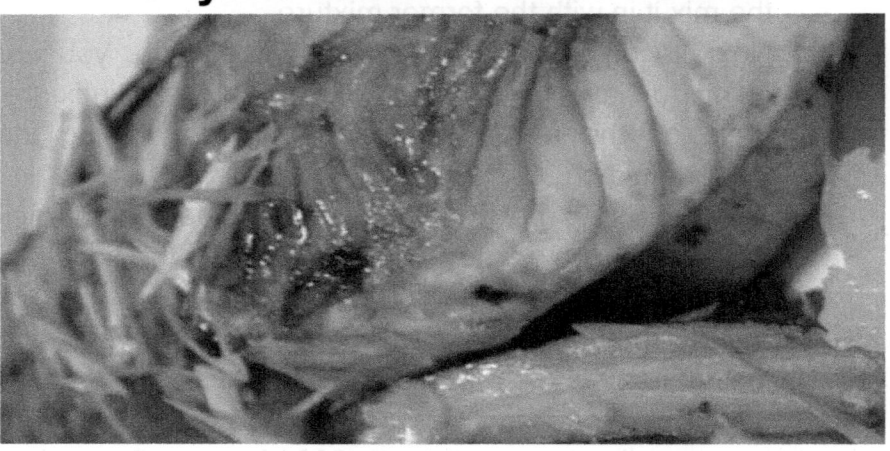

For all of the meat lovers out there, having a perfectly done steak is like a dream come true and it has never been easier now with Air Fryer! This particular dish is a marriage of the traditional recipe for steak along with the culture of Japan which as wrought upon the invention of Mirin (A form of Japanese cooking wine) to bring a marinate for halibut stake unlike no other that is bursting with flavor and awesomeness!

Portion

This particular recipe will help you create about servings for 3 persons.

Total Time

This recipe will take about 30 minutes of your cooking time, but with the preparation timing, it will take about 39-41 minutes in total.

Ingredients

- 1 pound of halibut steak

For Marinade:

- About 2/3 cup of low sodium soy sauce.
- ½ cup of Japanese cooking wine, also known as Mirin
- About a quarter cup of sugar
- 2 tablespoons of lime juice
- A quarter cup of orange juice
- A quarter teaspoon of crushed red pepper flakes
- A quarter teaspoon of grounded ginger
- Smashed garlic clove

Nutritional Values

- Calories : 280
- Fat : 7.4g
- Saturated Fat : 1.2g
- Carbohydrates : 14.1g
- Protein : 36.9g
- Cholesterol: 80mg

How to Make The Dish

- The most important part of this dish is the marinade sauce or the Teriyaki glaze. So, it is of utmost importance to prepare that first! Start off by bringing in all the ingredients of the teriyaki glaze into a saucepan.
- Bring the contents to a boil, then sequentially reduce the temperature by half and then cool it up.

- Once the marinade has cooled down, pour around half of the glaze into a bag enclosed with the halibut.
- Put it in a freezer and keep it there for at least 30 minutes.
- Now, it's time prepare your Ari Fryer! Take some time and pre-heat the Fryer to a temperature of 390 degrees Fahrenheit.
- Take out the halibut out from the fridge and gently place in the Air Fryer tray, from where you are to push it into the cooking chamber and let it stay there for around 10-12 minutes.
- Once it is done, brush the finalized dish with the rest of the glaze for extra added taste.
- Since this is going to be a lunch dish, it is wise to serve it over with a platter of white rice and if possible, a portion of mint chutney.

Chapter 4: Dinner Recipes

Meat Balls and Creamy Potatoes

Just the name of this dish is enough to make the taste buds of any person jump up and down! Two of your most favorite things in life, potatoes, and meat balls are combined together here in order to create a breathtaking and awe-inspiring recipe that is well deserved to be placed in your dinner table! These creamy potatoes are deeply drenched under milk and cheese to give you an extra dose of rich flavor.

Portion

This particular recipe will help you create about servings for 4-6 persons.

Total Time

This recipe will take about 40 minutes of your cooking time, about 25 minutes of which is allocated towards cooking the potato while the rest is allocated towards melting the cheese.

Ingredients

- 1 piece of white onion
- 12 ounces of lean grounded beef
- 1 tablespoon of freshly chopped parsley
- Half tablespoon of fresh thyme leaves
- 1 large egg
- 3 tablespoon of breadcrumbs
- 1 tablespoon of salt and pepper
- 7 medium sized peeled russet potatoes
- ½ cup of cream
- ½ cup of milk
- 1 tablespoon black pepper
- ½ tablespoon of nutmeg
- Half cup of grated gruyere cheese

Nutritional Values

- Calories : 435
- Fat : 24g
- Saturated Fat : 9g
- Carbohydrates : 30g
- Protein : 25g
- Cholesterol: 110mg

How to Make The Dish

- o The very first step into making this dish is to give a little effort into pre-heating your air-fryer to a minimum temperature of 199 degree Celsius or 390 degrees Fahrenheit.
- o While the Fryer is in pre-heat, come to the side and prepare the mixture consisting of the meat. Here you will need to finely mince the peeled and chopped

onions and mix them with the grounded meat, herbs, eggs, salt, breadcrumbs and pepper thoroughly in a bowl. Remember that you are not supposed to over the handle.
- Set that aside and then move on to prepare the other mixture comprising of the potato. A mandolin here is recommended to easily get the wafer-thin slices of potatoes that are required here, using that peel and slice the potatoes. After which gently take a bowl and whisk up the milk and cream, wait for some time and add extra seasonings. Take the slices of potatoes and dip them into them milky mixture to give it an even coating.
- Take a baking dish of a size of preferably 8 inch and finely layer the coated potatoes over it. Pour down any remaining milk which you might have over those potatoes and place the baking dish inside the cooking chamber and let the potatoes cook for about 25 minutes.
- You will get some extra time while the potatoes are being cooked, so here what you want to do is gently take the meat mixture and cramp them up in tiny shapes of mini meatballs, preferably grape sized. When the potatoes and fully cooked, then go ahead and create a layer of your meat balls on top of the potatoes. Finally, cover up the meat and potatoes with some finely shredded cheese for added taste, and place the whole dish inside the heating chamber for another 8 to 10 minutes until the whole package has finely wrapped itself up and the cheese has attained a tender brown molten brown texture.

Crab Cakes

Crabs are undoubtedly some of the most majestic creatures of the sea. They are small in size, yet very elegant in their nature of keeping themselves highly protected within their own fortress of solitude (Shell). Frying up such a majestic creature using this recipe that hails from Thailand might require a little bit labor, but the fragrance and taste that will come from your finally prepared dish will be tantalizing, to say the least!

Portion

This particular recipe will help you create about servings for 4-6 persons.

Total Time

This recipe will take about 40 minutes of your cooking time, about 25 minutes of which is allocated towards cooking the potato while the rest is allocated towards melting the cheese.

Ingredients

- About a Pound of Crab Meat
- 2 Nicely Beaten Egg Whites
- About a tablespoon of olive oil
- About a quarter of finely chopped red onion
- About a quarter of finely chopped red bell pepper
- 2 tablespoons of finely chopped celery
- About a quarter of finely chopped tarragon and chives
- About a half a teaspoon of chopped parsley
- About 1/4rth of a cup of mayonnaise
- About 1/4rth of a cup of sour cream
- A whole cup of all-purpose flour
- A whole cup of breadcrumbs
- About a teaspoon of Olive Oil
- About half a teaspoon of salt.

Nutritional Values (100gm)

- Calories : 265
- Fat : 17g
- Saturated Fat : 3.7g
- Carbohydrates : 9g
- Protein : 19g
- Cholesterol: 137mg

How to Make The Dish

- o The very essence of this dish requires a great level of panache to successfully pull this off, and a whole lot of depth and care goes into the making of this dish. The first step is to Cook all of the onions, celery and peppers in olive oil over medium heat in a sauté pan.

- Keep the ingredients under stress and let them sweat for about 4 or 5 minutes, or up until the point where they seem to look a bit translucent. Take off the mixture and keep it aside.
- Next, you are going to need to prepare the breading mix by taking all the breadcrumbs and putting them in a blender alongside the olive and oil and salt.
- Once the process is complete, put them gently in a bowl and crack opens the eggs and flour in separate bowls. Manage up your breading station and line all of the three bowls up.
- In another bigger bowl, take the crabmeats, mayonnaise, egg white, sour cream, spices and the sautéed vegetables to mix them up gently.
- Now it's time to fire up your fryer by pre-heating it to a temperature of around 390 degrees Fahrenheit.
- Take some good care and try to mold the mixture of crabs into patties or any shape to fulfill your heart's content.
- Gently dip and drench the patties into the flour, mix them up with egg and combine them with the breading mixture.
- Make sure to press the breading strongly unto your patty so that it has a nice consistency.
- Place the patties into a frying basket, and put the tray inside the cooking chamber and place it there for about 8-10 minutes until the crab patties have gained a very tender and brown texture.

Air Fried Spring Rolls

Asia is a continent that is well known for its mysterious and mostly delicious palettes of foods, especially in the frying department! And this recipe is no stranger to that fact! Using their signature Asian Noodles as the core ingredient, these Asian Spring Rolls have been made up to stand the test of time and compete with any other dinner dish on your table!

Portion

This particular recipe will help you create about servings for 5 persons.

Total Time

This recipe will take about 15 minutes of your cooking time, about 7 minutes of which is allocated towards preparation.

Ingredients

- About of 50 grams of genuine Asian Noodles
- About a tablespoon of sesame oil
- 200 grams of finely minced meat
- Finely minced small onions.
- About 3 cloves of garlic
- About 1 cup of either fresh or frozen vegetables.
- 1 tablespoon of soy sauce
- A pack of spring roll wrappers
- About 2 tablespoons of Cold Water.

Nutritional Values (100gm)

- Calories : 195
- Fat : 2.08g
- Carbohydrates : 36g
- Protein : 8.7g

How to Make The Dish

- Start off the crafting of your dish by first softening your Asian Noodles by soaking them in considerably hot water. Once they are softened enough, pick them up gently, drain them and soften up the noodles, cutting them up it's preferred sized.
- Next, take a wok and stir fry the meat, garlic, onion and mixed vegetables.
- Toss in the Soy sauce and gently pull up the mixture from the pan and pour it in with the already prepared (softened, cut) Asian noodles. You are to keep this mixture away for a few minutes to allow all of the flavors to slowly be absorbed by the noodles.
- Take the fillings and pour them inside the spring roll wrappers, filling them up starting from the middle.

- Tend to the sides of the spring roll, fold the wrapper so that contents does not come out.
- If needed, us a little bit of water to firmly secure the wrappers.
- Now, before starting to fry your rolls, you are going to have to pre-heat your Air Fryer to a temperature of about 360 degrees Fahrenheit or 182 degrees Celsius.
- Brush up the vegetable oils on each of the spring roll and place all of them in a finely placed single layer on your food tray.
- Next slowly push forwards the food tray into the cooking chamber and let them cook for about 8 minutes, and you are done!
- If you wish, then you can present your rolls with either a cocktail of sweet chili sauce or even Asian Dipping Sauce for added flavor!

Fish Nuggets

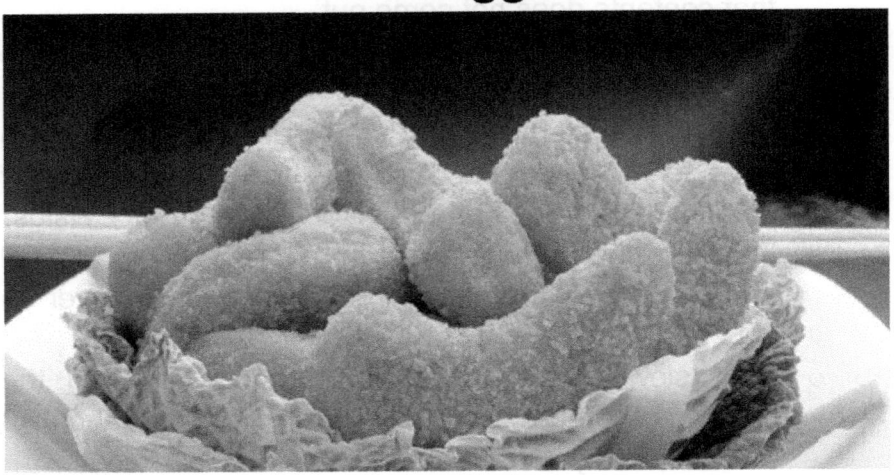

Who doesn't like Nuggets!? They are the singular most delicious source of chomping upon crispy and fried bite-sized chunks of tender and juicy meats! For those who want to experience something a little bit off the grid, these fish nuggets are exactly for them! These embrace the juicy tenderness of nuggets while replacing the traditional chicken meat with fish! A perfect dish to go along with the rice at your dinner table!

Portion

This particular recipe will help you create about servings for 4 persons.

Total Time

This recipe will take about 10 minutes of your cooking time.

Ingredients

- About a pound of fresh cod
- About 2 tablespoons of olive oil

- About half a cup of all-purpose flour
- 2 large sized whole eggs that are finely beaten.
- About 3 quarters of panko branded bread crumbs (or any bread crumbs will do)
- Salt as required

Nutritional Values (100gm)

- Calories : 380.2
- Fat : 95g
- Saturated Fat : 3.7g
- Carbohydrates : 6.5g
- Protein : 61.9g
- Cholesterol: 320.9mg

How to Make The Dish

- Step One for this dish, like many of the recipes which involve a certain degree of frying to be done in this recipe list, is to first take good care to pre heat your Air Fryer to a temperature of about 390 degrees Fahrenheit or a 198 Degree Celsius
- While the Fryer is being heated up, you are to come aside and prepare the mixture that you are going to be using as your breading, and for that take a food processor/ blender and put in the breadcrumbs, olive oil and salt. Fire up the blending process and keep blending them until they have reached a very fine state.
- After that step, you are going to need to prepare your breading lines by mixing up your breadcrumb mixture, flour, and eggs in individual bowls.
- Now it's time to prepare your Cod. Take the Cods and cut them up into about 1-inch thick slices of approximately 2 inches long.

- Next, take each of the fish sticks and deep them thoroughly into the flour put a layer of coating all over them.
- Next, take the coated sticks and dip them into the mixture of beaten eggs.
- Finally, coat up the egg soaked fish sticks now with a layer of breadcrumb mixture and keep firmly pressing it until the breading have fixated itself unto the fish.
- Jerk the covered fish sticks to shake off some of the excess breading.
- Next, place the fish sticks even in your cooking tray, at equal spaces distances to make it look a little bit fancier, and let it cook for about 8 to 10 minutes until the sticks have reached a beautiful golden brown texture.

Breaded Fish Fillets

Fishes are largely regarded all around the world as being an incorporated part of any healthy and balanced diet. They contain a very rich level of proteins and minerals while being substantially low in fat, making them very ideal consumes for people who likes to stay leaned towards a little bit on the healthy side of life. But even the healthiest person might sometimes prefer to have something that tastes good while being healthy at the same time! And this where these finely Air Fried Breaded Fish Fillets come in to accompany alongside you next dinner meal!

Portion

This particular recipe will help you create about servings for 2 persons.

Total Time

This recipe will take about 15 minutes of your cooking time. Most of the 12 minutes will be used up while cooking and the rest will be consumed while preparing the fish sticks for use.

Ingredients

- About 4 tablespoons of finely selected vegetable oil.
- Approximately 100 grams of breadcrumbs (more If required)
- One Fully whisked egg (whole)
- Around 4 pieces of fish fillets finely organized and cut into equal shapes.
- 1 piece of lemon finely sliced into wedges to be used during serving.

Nutritional Values (100gm)

- Calories : 380.2
- Fat : 95g
- Saturated Fat : 3.7g
- Carbohydrates : 6.5g
- Protein : 61.9g
- Cholesterol: 320.9mg

How to Make the Dish

- Even before starting off with your main preparation, what you will need to do is at first set your Air-Fryer to a pre-heating temperature of about 360 degrees Fahrenheit of 180 degree Celsius.
- While your Air Fryer Is being pre-heated, on the other side take a bowl and pour in the oil alongside the bread crumbs to create a good solution. You stir these two together until they break apart and form a mixture of loose crumbs.
- Take another completely separate bowl, take your large egg, crack it up into the bowl and pour it in, After which take some time to gently start whisking the egg,

slowly at first then gradually increasing your speed as you go.
- Once your whisking Is done, you are to grab the pieces of fish fillet and gently dip them into the beaten egg solution.
- Pull it up from the bowl, and shake it off until all of the excess egg has been dripped off.
- Then dip it again into the bread crumb and oil mixture until the body of the fillet has been fully coated with even finishing.
- Repeat this process for all of the fillets.
- Take out your cooking tray, lay down the fish fillets evenly with equal distanced spaces and push the cooking tray inside the cooking chamber and let them fry for about 12 minutes or until they have reached a beautiful golden brown texture.

Chapter 5: Desert Recipes

Chocolate Cake

When it comes to desert, Chocolate does indeed come first into the minds of people of all ages, and chocolate cake is undoubtedly the magnum opus of deserts all around the world! This recipe is focused on showing you how you can cook up a gorgeously delicious Chocolate Cake using your Air Fryer!

Portion

This particular recipe will help you create about servings for 8-10 persons.

Total Time

This recipe will take about 45 minutes of your cooking time, where you will be needed to be actively preparing it for about 15 minutes.

Ingredients

Cake:

- About 3 eggs
- Half cup of sour cream
- About a cup of flour
- About two-thirds of cup of caster sugar (either white or fine)
- About 9 tablespoons of unsalted butter.
- About 6 tablespoons of cocoa powder.
- About 1 teaspoon of baking powder.
- About half tea spoon of baking soda.
- About 2 teaspoons of vanilla

Chocolate Icing:

- About 5.5 ounces of chocolate
- About 3 and a half tablespoon of unsalted softened butter
- 1 and a two-third cup of icing sugar
- About 1 teaspoon of vanilla

Nutritional Values

- Calories : 371
- Fat : 15g
- Saturated Fat : 5g
- Carbohydrates : 53g
- Protein : 5g
- Cholesterol: 58mg

How to Make The Dish

- When it comes to baking, temperature is the most important aspect of it, and just like that to start baking

this cake, what you will need to do is initially pre-heat your Air Fryer to about 320 degree Celsius.
- After that, take all the ingredients of your cake and put them in a blender or a food processor and create a battery of admirable consistency.
- Next, place your dish into the table and pour down the batter into the dish. This dish will then be placed on top of your Air Fryers Tray, and the tray is then pushed inside the cooking chamber. Here you will need to set the timer of your Air Fryer to 35 minutes.

Pro Tip: What you can do here to check if the cake is cooked evenly, you can prick it a little bit using a stick. If the stick comes out clean, then your cake is done. If not, then you will need to set your Air fryer timer to just another 5 more minutes.

- Once your cake is done, bring out the basket from your cooking chamber and let the cake cool down for a while.
- On the other hand, you will need to create the molten chocolate for your cake. So , melt the Au Bain Marie or any other form of chocolate which you like in your Microwave oven, leave it to cool for a little while then mix up the icing ingredients alongside the molten chocolate.
- Finally, remove the now cooled cake from the dish and carefully place it on a plate. Decorate it and cover it with the chocolate icings which you prepared earlier and serve it well!

Apricot Blackberry Crumble

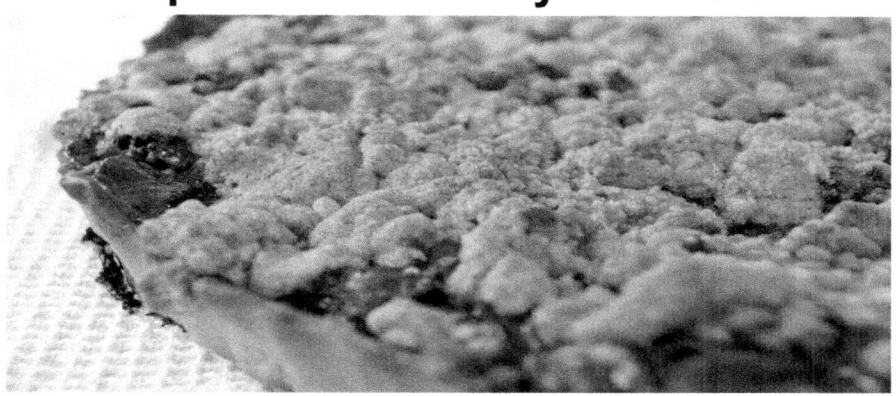

Are you missing the mouth-watering pies which your Grandmother used to bake for you whenever you went to your village or country side? This particular recipe is here to add a sense of nostalgia into you and help you to re-create that childhood memory in a delicious manner in the form of this Apricot Blackberry Crumble!

Portion

This particular recipe will help you create about servings for 6-8 persons.

Total Time

This recipe will take about 30 minutes of your cooking time, where you will be needed to be actively preparing it for about 10 minutes.

Ingredients

- About 18 ounces of fresh apricots
- About 5 and a half ounces of blackberries
- About ½ a cup of sugar

- 2 tablespoons of fresh lemon juice.
- Just a cup of flour
- Salt as required
- About 5 tablespoons of cooled butter

Nutritional Values

- Calories : 422
- Fat : 15g
- Saturated Fat : 9g
- Carbohydrates : 70g
- Protein : 5g
- Cholesterol: 41mg

How to Make the Dish

- The first which you will need to do here for the preparation of this recipe is to prepare the apricots by cutting them in half and removing the stones.
- Cut them up into small cubes and place them in a separate bowl alongside the blackberries, lemon juice and 2 table spoon of sugar and mix it thoroughly.
- When the mixture has reached a good level of consistency, scoop up the mixture and pour it down to your greased up oven dish.
- In another separate bowl, mix up the flour with just a little pinch of salt and the left over sugars.
- To that mixture, add the cooled butter and about 1 tablespoon of cold water and keep rubbing them together until you have a crumbly texture.
- Now before you are going to insert your baking tray into the cooking chamber of your Air Fryer, you are going to pre-heat the Fryer to 390 degrees Fahrenheit.
- Press the crumbly mixture evenly all over the fruits and keep pressing down ever so gently.

- Finally, place the oven inside the tray of your Air Fryer and push them inside the cooking chamber, allowing it to bake for about 20 minutes. At the end you will notice a gorgeous golden brown finish letting you know that the dish is done!

Vanilla Soufflé

There is always a constant battle going between food enthusiasts struggling for taking either vanilla or chocolate. We didn't want this book to also cause another flame war, so right after our chocolate recipe, this here is a very simply vanilla soufflé which you will be able to make using your Air Fryer as a desert to end your hard and long day with a smile in your face!

Portion

This particular recipe will help you create about servings for 6 persons.

Total Time

This recipe will take about 1 Hour 30 minutes of your cooking time, where you will be needed to be actively preparing it for about 20 minutes.

Ingredients

- About a quarter cup of all-purpose flour
- About a quarter of softened butter
- About 1 whole cup of milk
- About a quarter cup of sugar
- 2 teaspoons of vanilla extract
- 1 piece of vanilla bean
- About 5 egg whites
- About 4 egg yolks
- About 1 ounce of sugar
- About 1 teaspoon of tartar cream

Nutritional Values

- Calories : 129
- Fat : 2g
- Saturated Fat : 1g
- Carbohydrates : 25g
- Protein : 5g
- Cholesterol: 4mg

How to Make The Dish

- The first thing which you will need to do is mix up the flour and butter very thoroughly until it has reached a smooth consistency and has been turned into a paste.
- Take a sauce pan, and heat up the milk alongside dissolving the sugar. Here add the vanilla bean and bring the whole solution to a boil.
- To that very mixture, add the flour and butter and then using a wired whisk, beat it very thoroughly to make sure that no lumps are formed.
- You will have to simmer the whole mixture until it thickens, after which you will have to remove it from

the heat, toss out the vanilla bean and set up an ice bath and allow it to cool down for almost 10 minutes.
- Come to the side while the mixture is cooling down, and take about 6 pieces of 3 ounce ramekins and coat them up with butter and sprinkle alongside just a pinch of sugar.
- On the other hand, you will need another mixing bowl where you are going to quickly beat up the egg yolk and mix it up with the vanilla extract, combining it altogether with the milk mixture.
- On another bowl, you are going to crack open another egg and separate the whites, mix it up with sugar and tar tar cream and keep beating it until the egg white turns into a medium stiff peak.
- Take extra care into folding the egg white into the soufflé base and then pour into down into your baking dish.
- Before putting your dish into cooking tray and passing it inside the cooking chamber, you are going to pre heat the Air Fryer to about 330 degrees Fahrenheit and place 3 soufflé's at one time.
- The cooking time for this dish will be for 14-16 minutes. Repeat the process for the rest of your ramekins and sprinkle the powdered sugar on top of your soufflé and platter it with chocolate sauce on the side before serving!

Soft Chocolate Brownies With Caramel Sauce

Who can resist the soft temptation of a warm chocolate brownie that is dipped and drenched completely with a delicious caramel sauce? Make this desert in any party to become and make your audiences lick their fingers until the very last bite!

Portion

This particular recipe will help you create about servings for 4 persons.

Total Time

This recipe will take about 38 minutes of your cooking time, where you will be needed to be actively preparing it for about 20 minutes.

Ingredients

- About 125g of Caster Sugar
- About 2 tablespoons of Water
- About 142ml of Milk
- About 125g of Butter
- About 50g of Chocolate
- About 175g of Brown Sugar
- 2 Medium Sized Eggs, thoroughly Beaten
- About a 100g of Self Raising Flour
- About 2 Teaspoons of Vanilla Essence

Nutritional Values

- Calories : 190
- Fat : 14g
- Saturated Fat : 8g
- Carbohydrates : 20g
- Protein : 2g
- Cholesterol: 50mg

How to Make The Dish

- The first step which you are going to do in order to start the process of making these delicious brownies is to pre-heat your Air Fryer to 180 degrees Celsius.
- Now, it is time to first prepare your chocolate brownies. Melt about 100g of butter and chocolate on top of a bowl that is placed above a pan over medium level of heat.
- Toss in the brown sugar, eggs and vanilla essence alongside the raising flour and mix the whole mixture thoroughly and very well.
- After that, pour in the whole mixture into a greased dish suitable for the capacity of your Air Fryer.

- Push your dish inside the cooking chamber and allow it to cook for about 15 minutes keeping the temperature at 180 degree Celsius.
- While the brownies are cooking, you will have time to conjure up your caramel sauce! Mix up the caster sugar with water in a pan and keep that pan under medium heat until the sugar has completely melted up.
- After that, turn up the heat and cook everything until more three minutes until the sugar has achieved a light brown color.
- Turn down the heat and after just 2 minutes; add further the butter and keep the mixture stirring until the butter has completely melted down. Finally, slowly add a bit of butter.
- The hot caramel will take some time to cool, in the meantime take out the brownies from your Air Fryer and chop them up into even shaped squares!
- Serve them with a piece of banana and covering them up with your caramel sauce!

Mini Apple Pie

It is often said that an apple every day keeps the doctor away! While always eating the same kind of raw apple might get a little bit bland, even for the most health-conscious ones! This recipe will show you how to make your very own Apple Pie using your Air Fryer, to save yourself from the letting apple becomes just another mundane health product!

Portion

This particular recipe will help you create about servings for 9 persons.

Total Time

This recipe will take about 23 minutes of your cooking time, where you will be needed to be actively preparing it for about 5 minutes.

Ingredients

- About 75g of Plain Flour
- About 33g of Butter
- About 15g of Caster Sugar

- Water as Required
- 2 Medium Sized Red Apples
- Pinch Of Cinnamon
- Pinch Of Caster Sugar

Nutritional Values (Per 100gm)

- Calories : 237
- Fat : 11g
- Saturated Fat : 3.8g
- Carbohydrates : 34g
- Protein : 1.9g
- Cholesterol: 0mg

How to Make The Dish

- The first step to follow here before starting to bake the pie, is that you will need to pre-heat your Air Fryer to a temperature of about 180 Degree Celsius.
- Next, you focus will be on making the pastry. So for that, take a mixing bowl and place the flour and butter in it, rubbing the fat into the flour. Alongside that, toss in some sugar and mix the whole of the solution thoroughly. If needed, then you can also add some water to make the contents moist enough for them to be able to easily combine with each other.
- Once they have combined into nice dough, you will need to knead it until your dough gets a very consistent and smooth surface.
- Have a look at your muffin liners and oil them up with a littler butter to prevent the pastries from sticking themselves to the liners.
- Peel off the apple and dice them up. Now place the apples in the liners alongside a sprinkle of Cinnamon and Sugar.

- Repeat the same process and add another layer of pastry on top of the base layer, making sure to poke some holes using a fork to allow the pastries to breathe.
- Put the pastry liners into a tray and push it inside the Air Fryer cooking chamber and cook it there for 18 minutes to come up with the most perfect and healthy form of Apple Pie Imaginable!

Chapter 6 : Vegetables Recipes

Paneer and Cheese Balls

We already know what cheese is, for most of us, it is pretty much a part of our daily life. But what some of us might be unfamiliar with, it Paneer! So, let me educate you on that topic first. Paneer of simply called cottage cheese is one of India's more famous edible items that is made up of mostly milk. This item is extensively used amongst a wide range of international cuisines to make them both unique and delicious. If you are a vegetarian, then these Paneer and Cheese balls are going to go with any of your dishes amazingly, perhaps as a snack or even a side dish. If you have a party with small kids around the block, then don't hesitate and let these be the star of the show!

Portion

This particular recipe will help you create about servings for 4 persons.

Total Time

This recipe will take about 15 minutes of your cooking time, where you will be needed to be actively preparing it for about 5 minutes.

Ingredients

- About 200gm of grated Indian Cottage Cheese
- About 50gm of regular cheese of your choosing cut into tiny cubes.
- About 2 tablespoons of Flour
- About 1 tablespoon of Corn Flour
- 2 whole finely chopped onions
- 1 whole finely chopped ginger
- 1/3 tablespoon of Red Chili Powder
- Some finely chopped coriander leaves
- Cooking oil as required
- Salt as Required

Nutritional Values (Per 100gm)

- Calories : 1785
- Calorie From Fat: 840

How to Make The Dish

- The first step of this dish will focus on how you are going to prepare the stage for your Paneer and cheese balls. So firstly what you are going to do is take a medium sized bowl, and mix up all the required ingredients except Cheese and Oil. Take your time to mix them very thoroughly so that no lumps are created.

- After that, take a small portion of the whole mixture, stay calm and roll it up against your palm, turning it into a flat and circular shape if possible.
- Directly at the middle of your shape, take up one of the cheese cubes which you had set aside and place it there, stuff it finely.
- Once stuffed, slowly start to roll down the edges and turn the overall structure into a good looking healthy ball by rolling it on your palm, as if you are playing with dices.
- You are going to have to turn all of your mixtures into a ball, so a lot of work is ahead of you, take repeat the process until all of the mixtures has run out.
- Once you think that you are ready, Place the balls in your cooking tray, and insert the tray inside the cooking chamber of your Air Fryer and cook it up there for about 10-15 minutes at a temperature of 200 degree Celsius.
- Finally, serve the whole dish with delicious tomato ketchup and sweet or spicy chutney for extra taste.

Samosa

Hailing from the mysterious continent of India, Samosa's are tiny packages of extremely savory filings that can range from potatoes, peas, onions, noodles or even macaroni to fulfill the desires of any vegetarian out there! These are very easy to make, but pack some serious punch when it comes to delivering that delicious flavor which you demand!

Portion

This particular recipe will help you create about servings for 4 persons.

Total Time

This recipe will take about 15 minutes of your cooking time, where you will be needed to be actively preparing it for about 5 minutes.

Ingredients

- Oil
- About 2 cups of Flour
- About 1 teaspoon of Carom Seeds
- About 1 to 2 teaspoons of Molten Butter/Ghee
- 2 whole potatoes
- ½ a cup of Green Pea.
- About 2 teaspoons of Garam Masala Powder
- About 1 teaspoon of Ginger Garlic Paste
- About 1 teaspoon of Red Chili Powder
- About 1 teaspoon of Turmeric Powder.
- Salt as Required
- About ½ a teaspoon of Cumin Seeds.

Nutritional Values (Per 1 Piece)

- Calories : 308
- Fat: 18g
- Saturated Fat: 4g
- Cholesterol: 9mg
- Carbohydrate: 32g
- Dietary Fiber: 2g

How to Make The Dish

Stuffing

- The first thing which you are going to do for making the internal of your Samosa is to boil up 2 potatoes and add just 1 and a half cup of green pea in the water.
- Once the potatoes are boiled, mash them well.
- Take another bowl, put in the mashed potatoes alongside the peas and in that very bowl, add your

garam masala powder, red chili powder, turmeric powder, ginger garlic paste alongside as much salt as required. Make sure to mix them well properly.
- After that, take about 2 tablespoons of your oil and pour it down in your pan, gently letting it warm under medium flame. Here, add the cumin seeds and wait for the moment until the splutter.
- You will get a very nice and vibrant aroma that is your signal to pour the mixture which you had made earlier.
- Stir it for a few minutes, pour down the whole mixture in a bowl and keep it aside.

The Outer Shell

- Next up comes the coating and for this you take another bowl, drop down your flour, carom seeds, molten butter/ghee and some water to properly mix them up. Then knead them finely into proper dough.
- Take a regular wrapping cover and wrap up the dough for about 30 minutes.
- When you see that the dough has raised enough, take it out and cut them in shapes of the Samosa as shown in the picture, use your finger to prepare the pockets where you will fill in the samosa with your mixture.

The Frying

- Once you have prepared your stuffed samosa, brush them up with a little bit of oil.
- Turn on your Air Fryer and pre-heat for about 5 minutes and in 180 degree Celsius temperature.
- Keep it placed inside it, and let it cook for at least 18-20 minutes; you will get a nice texture of brown color letting you know that the frying is complete.

Vegetable Spring Rolls

Who doesn't love Spring Rolls!? These are perhaps one of the easiest ways to cater your child with vegetable, even if they are not interested in taking vegetables! Spring rolls are just that much delicious! And with your Air Fryer, you will be able to make them even healthier!

Portion

This particular recipe will help you create about servings for 8 Persons

Total Time

This recipe will take about 15 minutes of your cooking time, where you will be needed to be actively preparing it for about 5 minutes.

Ingredients

Stuffing:

- About 2 cups of shredded cabbage
- About 1 big sized Carrot
- About 2 big sized onions
- About ½ a Capsicum
- 2 inch cut pieces of Ginger
- 8 pieces of Garlic
- A considerable amount of Sugar
- About 1 tablespoon of pepper
- About 1 teaspoon of Soy Sauce
- Salt as Required
- 2 tablespoons of Cooking Oil
- A Little bit of Spring Onion as Garnish

The Outer Covering:

- About 10 pieces of Spring Roll Sheets
- About 2 tablespoons of Corn Flour
- Water as required

Nutritional Values (Per 100gm)

- Calories : 154
- Fat: 8g
- Saturated Fat: 1.2g
- Cholesterol: 1mg
- Carbohydrate: 4.3g
- Dietary Fiber: 2.4g

How to Make The Dish

- The first step which you are going to follow for making this dish is to take out your spring roll sheets from the

freezer and let it defrost outside for about an hour, and within that hour you are going to prepare your internal stuffing.
- Take the cabbage thinly grate it.
- Take the onion and carrots, cutting them into thin strips.
- The capsicum is to be sliced thinly.
- Chop up the ginger very with high precision and finesses.
- Try to ensure that all of the materials are of even and small thickness to achieve a shorter cooking time.
- Take a pan, and pour in the oil followed by all of your prepared vegetables, and sauté them, gradually adding pinches of salt and sugar. The sugar here is not mainly for taste, but rather to help the vegetable maintain a consistent color. Keep doing this in high flame for about 2 to 3 minutes.
- Once they seem to be cooked, add in your soya sauce and black pepper, stir and mix them well before switching off the flame.
- Garnish them up with just the right amount of onions to finish off your stuffing.
- Take a considerably sized bowl and add in the flour and water to make a creamy paste.
- By now the spring roll sheets are bound to be ready for use, so take a sheet and cut them up into sizes of your personal specification.
- Take about a tablespoon of your prepared stuffing and place them gently at one corner of your sheet, and then roll them up nicely adding some corn flour paste to make sure that it sticks.
- Repeat the same procedure until all of your ingredients has been used up.

- Now it's time for the frying! Pre heat your Air Fryer to about 180 degree Celsius for at least 5 minutes and arrange your rolls in the tray, oiling them up with a brush.
- Set the clock to a time of 20 minutes and temperature to 180 degree Celsius, and bake them for the next 10 minutes. Carefully take out the dish, flip the rolls and bake for another 10 minutes to ensure that both sides are being fried properly. Check for the color and texture, if you are happy with it, and then serve them warm and hot! If not, then let them bake for another 2 or 3 minutes until the desired color has been achieved.

Semolina Cutlets

Cutlets have turned into a staple part of a vegetarian's diet, and he/she naturally develops the tendency to try out various kinds of cutlets because they provide a fine balance between a healthy punch and delicacy. These Semolina cutlets are no exception, as they are packed with healthy goodness along with a pinch of rich flavors from all of your favorite vegetables!

Portion

This particular recipe will help you create about servings for 2 Persons

Total Time

This recipe will take about 15 minutes of your cooking time, where you will be needed to be actively preparing it for about 5 minutes.

Ingredients

- About 1 cup of Semolina
- About 5 cups of Milk
- About ½ cup of Refined Oil
- About 1 and a half cup of your favorite vegetables (usually Cauliflower, Carrot, Peas, Beans, Capsicum are used)
- Salt and Pepper as required

Nutritional Values (Serving of 252g)

- Calories : 327
- Fat: 1.2g
- Saturated Fat: 0.2g
- Cholesterol: 0mg
- Carbohydrate: 66.2g
- Dietary Fiber: 4.8g
- Protein: 12.1g

How to Make the Dish

- The very first step for making this dish is to take a pan and pour in the milk to heat it up. Once you are observe a good rise in temperature, toss in all the vegetables and cook all of them for about 2 or 3 minutes until the vegetables seem to become soft in nature. Afterwards, toss in amounts of salt and black pepper as required.
- Once that is done, add up the Semolina and cook them up for about 10 minutes until it seems to have thickened enough to expand beyond the pan.
- Take a plate and grease it up well, finely spread the whole mixture on top of the plate and allow it to refrigerate for the next 3-4 hours.

- Once done, bring out the frozen stuff and gently piece them out using a knife into your desired shape and sizes. Once done, coat them up with a little oil, and arrange them finely in your Air Fryer dish.
- Put the dish inside your Pre-Hearted Fryer and keep them for 10 minutes at a temperature of 180 degrees.
- Serve them up amongst your friend and family mates with some hot sauce!

Onion Pakora

Pakora, or often referred to being called "Pakoda" is a very delicious fried item which has its roots originated in India. These bite sized delicacies are fully packed with the goodness and richness of vegetable flavorings accompanied by a crispy flavor to keep your body and taste buds happy!

Portion

This particular recipe will help you create about servings for 6 Persons

Total Time

This recipe will take about 20 minutes of your cooking time, where you will be needed to be actively preparing it for about 5 minutes.

Ingredients

- About a cup of Gram Flour
- About 1/4rth a cup of Rice Flour

- About 2 teaspoons of Oil
- 4 whole pieces of Onion
- 2 whole pieces of Green Chili
- About 1 tablespoon of Coriander
- About ¼ teaspoon of Carom
- About 1/8th teaspoon of Chill powder
- Salt as required

Nutritional Values (Serving of 1)

- Calories : 119
- Fat: 2g
- Saturated Fat: 0g
- Cholesterol: 0mg
- Carbohydrate: 21g
- Dietary Fiber: 6g
- Protein: 6g

How to Make the Dish

- The first step for this dish is to go ahead and slice up your onions to very fine shapes.
- Next, bring the green chilies to the table and chop them up into small sizes as well.
- After that, cut up the Coriander into finely equal shaped sizes.
- Take a separate bowl and pour down the gram flour and rice flour followed by the addition of oil.
- Mix them up well properly and further add your turmeric powder, salt, chili powder, and Carom.
- After that, add the onions, Coriander, and chilies to the above mixture and mix them up very thoroughly adding just a few drops of water to achieve a good level of consistency.

- Finally, roll them up into tiny ball shapes.
- Now, it's time for the frying. Pre-heat your Air Fryer to about 200 degree Celsius for at least 5 minutes.
- Take you dish and arrange the vegetable balls justly, then push your tray inside the cooking chamber and fry them up for 8 minutes.
- After about 6 minutes, take it out and check if the balls have obtained a good level of brown coloration and texture, if not push them in for another few minutes.
- Serve them hot and with sauce!

Chapter 7 : High Protein Recipes

Chimichurri Skirt Steak

Also referred to as the mighty Fajita Steak in some continents, this particular dish which might resemble the shape of a weight lifter's shiny belt is actually a skirt of juicy and delicious steaky goodness! This dish is capable of fulfilling the demands of your rich flavor palette, as well as punching you in with a very heavy dose of protein!

Portion

This particular recipe will help you create about servings for 2 Persons

Total Time

This recipe will take about 35 minutes of your cooking time, where you will be needed to be actively preparing it for about 15 minutes.

Ingredients

- About 1 pound of Skirt Steak

For Chimichurri:

- About 1 cup of finely chopped parsley
- About 1/4rth cup of finely chopped mint
- About 2 tablespoons of finely chopped oregano
- 3 pieces of finely chopped garlic clove
- About a teaspoon of crushed red-pepper
- About 1 tablespoon of grounded cumin
- About 1 teaspoon of cayenne pepper
- About 2 teaspoons of smoked paprika
- About 1 teaspoon of salt
- About 1/4rth teaspoon of black pepper
- About 3/4rth cup of olive oil
- About 3 tablespoons of red wine vinegar

Nutritional Values (Serving of 1)

- Calories : 880
- Fat: 58g
- Saturated Fat: 10g
- Cholesterol: 0mg
- Carbohydrate: 43g
- Dietary Fiber: 10g
- Protein: 49g

How to Make the Dish

- The first step here that you are going to follow is to combine the ingredients that listed specifically for the Chimichurri in a separated mixing bowl.
- After that, you are to take your steak and cut them up into 2 portions of 8 ounce pieces and seal up them in a re-sealable bag alongside just ¼rth cup of the Chimichurri. Freeze them up for somewhere between 2 hours and 24 hours.
- When you are in the mood to cook, try to take out the refrigerated products at least 30 minutes before starting your session.
- Take some time to pre-heat your Air Fryer to a temperature of 390 degrees Fahrenheit and toss in the steaks into the cooking tray.
- Put the cooking tray inside the cooking chamber and cook them up for 8-10 minutes for a medium rare finish.
- Finally, garnish your dish with just 2 tablespoons of Chimichurri on top of them before serving and serve to delight!

Salmon With Dill Sauce

If you are looking for a fantastic way to serve your highly filled with protein salmon in a fancy way! Then serving them with a marinated Dill Sauce might just be what you are looking for! The Fresh Salmon finely numbers itself up within your taste buds and the cream sauce just adds enough seasoning to provide an exciting taste, while being careful about not overpowering the fragile flavor of the Salmon.

Portion

This particular recipe will help you create about servings for 4 Persons

Total Time

This recipe will take about 30 minutes of your cooking time, where you will be needed to be actively preparing it for about 15 minutes.

Ingredients

The Salmon:

- About 1 and a half pound of Salmon
- About 2 teaspoons of Olive Oil
- About 1 pinch of salt

The Dill Sauce:

- About half a cup of non-fat Greek yogurt.
- About ½ a cup of sour cream
- 1 pinch of salt
- About 2 tablespoons of finely chopped up dill

Nutritional Values (Serving of 1)

- Calories : 255.7
- Fat: 9.9g
- Saturated Fat: 3.3g
- Cholesterol: 0mg
- Carbohydrate: 106.6mgg
- Dietary Fiber: 0.2g
- Protein: 37.3g

How to Make the Dish

- For this dish, the temperature is very much important and should be kept in check while preheating, as just a slight change in your temperature might bring drastic changes to the flavorings. That being said, the first step here is to take your time and pre-heat your Air Fryer to about 270 degrees Fahrenheit.
- After which, cut off your Salmon into four 6 ounce pieces and drizzle them up with 1 teaspoon of olive oil.

- Then season them up with just a good amount of salt as required and place then place your salmon on top of the cooking dish.
- Place the salmon inside your cooking chamber and cook it up for around 20 to 23 minutes.
- On the side, prepare you to dill sauce by mixing up the yogurt, cream, chopped up Dill alongside required amount of salt in a separate mixing bowl and top it off with a wonderful garnishing of some more finely chopped up dill!

Cajun Shrimp

Hailing from French-speaking people of Acadia, Cajun spices stands as being one of their prime delicacies when flavoring up various meals by injecting them up with a barrage of spicy flavors! We all love shrimp because of its immense protein value and all the health benefits, but some of us might find the flavor of the ordinary regular shrimp to be a little bit bland! That is exactly where this recipe comes in, bringing you a beautiful marriage between the proteins of Shrimp and the Spices of Cajun.

Portion

This particular recipe will help you create about servings for 4 Persons

Total Time

This recipe will take about 10 minutes of your cooking time, where you will be needed to be actively preparing it for about 5 minutes.

Ingredients

- About1 and quarter pound of fierce tiger shrimp which counts to around 16-20 pieces
- About a quarter of cayenne pepper
- Half a teaspoon of old bay seasoning
- Quarter a teaspoon of smoked paprika
- About a pinch of salt
- About 1 tablespoon of Olive Oil

Nutritional Values (Serving of 1)

- Calories : 255.7
- Fat: 9.9g
- Saturated Fat: 3.3g
- Cholesterol: 0mg
- Carbohydrate: 106.6mgg
- Dietary Fiber: 0.2g
- Protein: 37.3g

How to Make the Dish

- Making this high-protein dish is pretty easy actually! The first step for this is to pre-heat your Air Fryer to a temperature of 390 degrees Fahrenheit.
- Next, inside a separate mixing bowl, take up all the ingredients required for coating the shrimp alongside the oil and spices and mix them up well.

- After that, arrange the shrimp in the cooking dish and make sure that gently place the cooking dish inside the cooking chamber of your Air Fryer.
- Cook it up inside the chamber for about 5 minutes, and you are done!
- To get the best flavor of this dish, it is recommended to serve it to your audiences with a side of rice.

Paprika Roast Chicken With Crispy Potato Rosti

This recipe is the perfect marriage of a delicious paprika coated Chicken Roast with the ingeniously crafted Swiss dish called " Rosti " that works magnificently in conjunction to create not only one of the healthiest dish but also a dish with the highest protein count possible! This recipe is one for the history books!

Portion

This particular recipe will help you create about servings for 2 Persons

Total Time

This recipe will take about 45 minutes of your cooking time, where you will be needed to be actively preparing it for about 10 minutes.

Ingredients

- 2 pieces of Chicken Leg
- About 2 teaspoons of Sweet Smoked Paprika
- 1 teaspoon of Honey
- Salt As Required
- Pepper As Required
- ½ a teaspoon of garlic powder

The Rosti:

- 1 whole sweet potato, finely peeled and roughly grated
- 1/4rth of a savoy cabbage, again, finely sliced
- 1 whole egg
- Salt as required
- Black Pepper as required
- 1 tablespoon of flour
- About 1 tablespoon of fresh parsley
- About ½

Nutritional Values (Serving of 1)

- Calories : 808
- Fat: 33.2g
- Saturated Fat: 8.7g
- Cholesterol: 353mg
- Carbohydrate: 5.3mg
- Dietary Fiber: 1.8g
- Protein: 115.7g

How to Make the Dish

- To start making this insanely high protein food, the first thing which you are going to need to do is pre-heat your Air Fryer to about 200 degree Celsius and let it

stay there for a few minutes until you have prepared your chicken.
- While it is being pre-heated, you are to mix up the paprika with honey and garlic powder, alongside just the right amount of salt and pepper added to the mix. Make sure to score the skin of the chicken properly and thoroughly rub it with the paprika mix.
- Since the process which you are going to utilize is an Air Frying process, you are not going to need any oil, just gently arrange the chicken inside the cooking tray and place the cooking tray upon your cooking chamber. Let it Air Fry for around 35 minutes until the skin looks to be crispy and bubbling.
- Once done, rest the chicken on a foil covered plate which you go ahead and prepare the rosti.
- To make the rosti, what you are going to do first is drain the grated up sweet potatoes of all the water using a kitchen towel to make them completely dry.
- Now, mix them up with cabbage, salt, egg, flour, pepper and parsley in a bowl.
- Shape the whole structure into two huge or 4 small sized rosti, depending on your preference and brush them up with olive oil, remember to use just a very tiny amount.
- Finally, Air Fry the rosti for about eight minutes, keeping in mind that you will need to turn it in-between to make sure that both sides have been thoroughly cooked achieving a golden brown texture.
- Remove the Rosti from the pan and serve it with a dash of light tomato salad and the prepared chicken.

Roast Potatoes With Bacon and Garlic

Bacon is well sought all around the world, known for its high protein content and energizing carbohydrate count! This recipe combines these factors from combine and merges them with the delightful flavor of roasted potatoes and garlic to create a very invigorating blend of relish.

Portion

This particular recipe will help you create about servings for 4 Persons

Total Time

This recipe will take about 30 minutes of your cooking time, where you will be needed to be actively preparing it for about 10 minutes.

Ingredients

- About 4 pieces of peeled and halved potatoes
- About 6 cloves of unpeeled garlic

- About 4 squashed rasher streaky bacon
- 2 roughly cut sprigs
- 1 tablespoon of rosemary

Nutritional Values (Serving of 1)

- Calories : 321.4
- Fat: 17.3g
- Saturated Fat: 5.7g
- Cholesterol: 25.7mg
- Carbohydrate: 34.7mg
- Dietary Fiber: 3.5g
- Protein: 37g

How to Make the Dish

- For this dish, the first thing which you are going to need to do is take your potatoes, rosemary, garlic and place in a bowl alongside the bacon. Make sure to mix them very thoroughly.
- After which, take some time to heat up pre-heat your Air-Fryer to a temperature of 200 degree Celsius, and on the side place everything on a cooking dish.
- Put the cooking dish inside the cooking chamber of your Air Fryer and let it roast there for around 25 to 30 minutes until it has reached a fine golden brown texture, letting you that it is done and ready to be served!

Chapter 8: Few More Interesting Bonus Recipes!

Panko Crusted Fish Fillet With Chips

Anything and Everything, once fried immediately increases its flavor palate in the deliciousness department, and fishes are no exception! While fishes themselves are already very healthy, sometimes frying those up might offend some people who are trying to stay more on the healthy sides. Using Panko Breadcrumbs, you will be able to make fried fishes that are much more lighter and in turn, more healthier while attaining the same great taste. These fishes taste even more awesome when coupled with the tartar sauce and French fries as a side snack!

Portion

This particular recipe will help you create portions for 2 people.

Total Time

This recipe will take about 40 minutes to cook. Of which about 35 minutes will be dedicated towards cooking, and the rest will be required for preparation.

Ingredients

The various components of this dish require individual amounts of ingredients to be made properly

The Fish:

- About 200 gram of Panko Breadcrumbs
- 1 teaspoon of Salt
- Just a pinch of Pepper
- About 2 tablespoons of finely chopped fresh parsley
- About 200 gram of Fish Fillet
- About 100gra of Generic Plain Flour
- 2 Whole Eggs

For The Chips:

- 2 Pieces Of big Maris Piper Potatoes (Peeled and Cut Into shapes of 1cm thick chips)
- 1 tablespoon of vegetable oil
- Salt as required
- Pepper as required

Tartar Sauce:

- About 200ml Mayonnaise

- About 2 tablespoons of Drained and Chopped Capers
- About 2 tablespoons of Gherkins or as an alternative, Jalapeno
- 1 finely chopped shallot
- About 4 tablespoons of finely chopped and squeezed lemon juice
- About 4 tablespoons of freshly chopped parsley
- Just a pinch of chili flakes
- Salt as required
- Black Pepper as required

Nutritional Values

- Calories : 215
- Fat : 8g
- Saturated Fat : 206g
- Carbohydrates : 3g
- Protein : 33g
- Sodium 40mg
- Dietary Fiber : 0g
- Cholesterol : 74mg

How to Make The Dish

- Crafting out this dish a very good amount of precision in the temperature department, because temperature fluctuations can be the cause of completely ruining this dish for you. Keeping that in mind, start off the preparation of this dish by making sure that you have fired up your Air Fryer and pre-heated it to a temperature of 200 degree Celsius and kept it at that temperature for at least 3 minutes.

- Take a separate bowl and mix up all the breadcrumbs, salt, pepper and parsley and thoroughly ensure that they are combined together properly
- Now, the time comes to prepare your fishes. First take the long whole fish, and carefully cut them into 4 long pieces resembling the likes the big fish fingers found in McDonalds
- Once you are done with that, place the large pieces of your fish on a plate
- Take separate bowls, in the first bowl, crack the eggs and properly whisk them until fine.
- On another plate, pour down the flour and on another one, drop down the breadcrumb mix which you prepared early on in this tutorial.
- Now, carefully take up a large piece of cut fish and follow the sequence, first dip them in the flour, then dip them in the egg and finally mix them with the breadcrumbs. Make sure that they are fully coated, and the whole of their both sides are evenly covered. Press gently with your fingers to ensure maximum stability.
- Keep repeating this process until all of the fishes have been prepared.
- Once done, Open up your Air Fryer and take out the cooking dish, gently lay down all of your fishes on the cooking tray and place the tray inside the cooking chamber, let it be there for about 15 minutes or until the fishes have reached a golden brown texture.
- Take them out, and cover the fishes with foil to keep them warm while you prepare the chips on the side.
- Take your chips, Pat them dry with a paper towel and then shake them gently in oil. After which, bring out the cooking dish once more and place the fries inside your cooking chamber, keeping them there for 20 minutes.

Keep in mind that for even cooking, you will need to shake the fries twice during the session, apply seasonings.
- Finally, mix up all the ingredients in a bowl for the sauce, and serve it for yumminess!

Panko Crusted Fish Fillet With Chips

"Pakoda" or Bhaji's are more of a staple food that hails from the sub-continent of India, these dishes tend to be around the lunch/dinner tables and also sometimes in a large gathering as a snack. Healthy and extremely delicious, Onion Bhaji's are in general consumed with a garnish of ketchup or with a savory curry of dal (Lentils)

Portion

This particular recipe will help you create portions for 2 people.

Total Time

This recipe will take about 60 minutes to cook. Of which about 40 minutes will be dedicated towards cooking, and the rest will be required for preparation.

Ingredients

The various components of this dish requires individual amounts of ingredients to be made properly

The Dal:

- 1 piece of Onion
- 1 piece of finely diced Garlic Clove
- ! piece of finely chopped chili
- Gingers chopped up into 1 inch pieces
- 1 tablespoon of vegetable oil
- About 2 stems of curry leaves
- 1 teaspoon of turmeric powder
- About 1 teaspoon of garam masala
- About 1 tea spoon of yellow mustard seed
- 75 grams of red lentils
- One 400 gram tin of tomatoes
- 50 gram of unsweetened desiccated coconut

Raita:

- Take about ½ a cucumber
- Freshly squeeze juice of 1 lemon
- 1 small bunch of freshly cut mint
- 100 gram of natural yoghurt

Bhaji:

- About 90 gram of chick pea flour
- About 1 teaspoon of cumin seeds
- About ½ teaspoon of turmeric
- About ½ teaspoon of fennel seeds
- About ½ teaspoon of salt
- About 1 whole finely chopped chili

- Gingers chopped into 1 inch pieces
- About 2 pieces of grated garlic cloves
- About ½ of a small lemon juice
- A small bunch of fresh coriander finely chopped
- About 2 thinly sliced onions.

Nutritional Values

- Calories : 350
- Fat : 27g
- Saturated Fat : 3g
- Carbohydrates : 0g
- Protein : 0g
- Sodium 2,000mg
- Dietary Fiber : 0g
- Cholesterol : 0mg

How to Make The Dish

Since there are various components to this recipe, we will be tackling each of them separately, starting with the very basic element of the recipe that is the curry or "Dal if you will.

- o Start preparing the dal by taking a medium sized pan and pouring down a good amount of oil as required, keep it under flame and mix in the onion, garlic, chili and ginger to sweat them for the next 10 minutes. After that, turn up the heat a little more and add the curry leaves, turmeric, mustard seeds and garam masala. Fry a further one minute and then add all the lentils.
- o Keep stirring the whole mixture until everything is evenly distributed and coated, after which toss in the tomatoes and coconut. Apply your seasoning and cover it up to let it simmer for the next 40 minutes, or

at least until the lentils have become tender. If they seem to have become a little bit drier than expected, then add some extra water to create a soupier dal.
- With the dal done, next, we move on to the raita. This is fairly straightforward, and all you will need to do is first cut up the watery core out of the cucumbers and very finely cut out the flesh, causing minimal damage. After which, add in some lemon juice alongside mint, cucumber and the yoghurt mixing them up good with a pinch of salt to taste. Once everything is in, stir them up properly.
- Next in line comes the bhaji mix, for this one you will need to take a reasonably large bowl and drop down the flour, alongside enough water so that the whole mixture turns into a thick paste resembling a double cream.
- On the side, take in the cumin, fennel, and turmeric in a frying pan and toast them out for about a minute, followed by the addition of salt, ginger, chili and garlic for added taste.
- For the final stage of this recipe, go ahead and pre-heat your Air Fryer to a temperature of about 180 degree Celsius.
- On the side, take the bhaji mix and add the lemon juice, onions, and coriander leaves, mix them up until thoroughly coated.
- Wet your hands a little bit and take large portions of the bhaji mix, to ball them up into sizes of olives.
- Take out your cooking tray, flatten them down just a little bit and arrange them in the tray, after that push the tray into the cooking chamber and let them fry for no more than 10 minutes or until they start to show a crispy golden texture.

- Serve the yummy balls with the prepared raita and dal for extra added taste on the side.

Vegetable Crisps and Cheesy Pesto Twist

Some people, especially kids don't like to eat vegetables, and as a result, they miss out on some of the most crucial and important nutrient values require by the human body to stay healthy and fit. This recipe is aimed to be a solution to that problem, presenting the benefits of the vegetables in the form of healthy and delicious crisps! That is coupled with Cheesy Pesto Twists, making this an irresistible and piquant Air Fryer creation.

Portion

This particular recipe will help you create portions for 4 persons.

Total Time

This recipe will take about 50 minutes to cook. Of which about 40 minutes will be dedicated towards cooking, and the rest will be required for preparation.

Ingredients

The various components of this dish requires individual amounts of ingredients to be made properly

The Vegetable Crisps:

- About 2 pieces of parsnips
- About 2 beetroots
- 1 medium sized peeled sweet potato
- About 1 tablespoon of Olive Oil
- About ½ teaspoon of chili powder / herbs de Provence

The Cheesy Pestos:

- 1 x 320 gram pack of all butter puff pastry
- About 1 tablespoon of Flour
- About 50 gram of cream cheese
- About 4 tablespoons of Pesto
- 1 whole egg (properly beaten)
- 50 grams of grated Parmesan Cheese

Nutritional Values

Vegetable Crips

- Calories : 473
- Fat : 23g
- Saturated Fat : 1.8g
- Carbohydrates :60g
- Protein : 5g

- Sodium 966mg
- Dietary Fiber :4.7g
- Cholesterol : 0mg

Vegetable Crips

- Calories : 290
- Fat : 10g
- Saturated Fat : 3.5g
- Carbohydrates :40g
- Protein : 10g
- Sodium 460gm
- Dietary Fiber :2g
- Cholesterol : 10mg

<u>How to Make The Dish</u>

- o The very first step of this savory dish to pre-heat is to take a step back and pre-heat your Air Fryer to a temperature of 240 degree Celsius.
- o Take up a good quality peeler and shave up all the parsnips, beetroots, and sweet potatoes to super-thin strip sizes. Once done, toss in all the vegetable slices in the oil alongside the chili powder/herbs. Finally, season them up with salt and pepper as required.
- o Once done, take out your cooking dish and arrange them nice in a tray after which you are to push the tray inside the cooking chamber and let it cook for the next 20 minutes or until they have reached a fine golden texture. Make sure to shake the pan halfway through the process.
- o Now, for the cheesy Pesto twist, what you will need to do first is prepare the pastry by rolling them up into a rectangle on top of a surface, making sure that it was lightly floured as to avoid stickiness. The vertical side

should be long while the horizontal side should be short.
- Cut the whole thing down the middle and spread finely the cream and cheese and pesto over around one half of the pastry, and then take the other half of the pastry to cover it up, making a sandwich of sort.
- Once done, cut them down in the middle once more to create 2 long rectangles and slice each of them into 1 cm thick horizontal strips.
- Finally, take the pastry strips and twist them gently to lengthen them up, keep repeating this process until all of them are done.
- On a separate bowl, cracks open an egg, take the twists and dip then in the egg before sprinkling bits of parmesan cheese on top of them.
- Once they are ready, take out your cooking dish from the Air Fryer, put the twists in the tray and push them forward inside the cooking chamber, letting them cook for about 20-25 minutes, until they have gained a fine golden brown texture.

Thai Roast Beef Salad With Nam Jim Dressing

Thailand is well known for creating some of the most awe-inspiring and tangy flavored sauces available on the planet! Hailing from the lands of Thailand, the Nam Jim sauce that is accompanied by this perfectly medium rare roasted beef is a prime example of how a combination of a myriad of flavors should be implemented that includes a whole range of salty, sweet, spicy and sour palate. Follow this dish and use your Air Fryer to experience a ting of Thai.

Portion

This particular recipe will help you create portions for 2 persons.

Total Time

This recipe will take about 60 minutes to cook. Of which about 50 minutes will be dedicated towards cooking, and the rest will be required for preparation.

Ingredients

The various components of this dish require individual amounts of ingredients to be made properly

Beef:

- 1 kg of the topside of Beef
- 1 tablespoon of olive oil
- Salt and Pepper as required

Salad:

- 1 whole grated Carrot
- ½ of a small grated white cabbage
- 1 red very finely sliced red pepper
- A small handful of sugar snap peas (Chopped)
- A Small handful of beansprouts
- About 2 teaspoons of toasted sesame seeds
- A Small bunch of chopped coriander leaves

Dressing:

- About 2 tablespoon of fish sauce
- About 2 tablespoons of fresh lime juice
- About 2 pieces of Red Bird's eye chili
- About 2 pieces of garlic cloves
- 1 inch pieces of ginger
- About 2 tablespoons of tamari sauce
- About 2 tablespoons of sesame oil

- About 4 tablespoons of water
- About 1 tablespoon of palm sugar
- 2-3 chopped up small
- Chopped up stems of coriander
- A dash of salt

Nutritional Values

- Calories : 170
- Fat : 6g
- Saturated Fat : 1.7g
- Carbohydrates :0g
- Protein : 29g
- Sodium 57mg
- Dietary Fiber :0g
- Cholesterol : 86mg

How to Make The Dish

- The first thing which you will need to do is prepare your Air Fryer beforehand by heating it up to a maximum temperature for a few minutes while you on the side you take the necessary steps to prepare the beef.
- While the Air Fryer is being pre-heated, take your beef and rub it up with oil, marinate it with salt and pepper as required.
- Take out the cooking tray from your Air Fryer, and arrange the beef in the dish, after which push the tray into the Air Fryer and let it roast for the next 30 minutes, making sure to turn down the temperature to 190 degree Celsius after a span of 10 minutes. Once done, this is going to give you a medium rare statured meat which is ideal for this particular dish.

- While is the roast is getting ready, you can turn your head towards the preparation of the Salad by tossing in all the ingredients together.
- As for the Nam Jim Dressing, You will need to put all the ingredients specified for the Nam Jim into a food blender and thoroughly blitz it for about a minute or two. Make sure that the whole dressing is properly combined with a thin consistency.
- Drizzle the dressing over your salad and store the rest if you want, for when you might need them in the future.
- By now, the beef should be ready, take it out and allow it rest for the next 20 minutes to make sure that it's extremely juicy! Cut it up into thin wafer thick slices and serve it up with the dressed salad on the side.
- Garnish them up with Coriander and toasted peanuts/lime wedges if you want!

Salmon With Creamy Courgette

Portion

This particular recipe will help you create portions for 2 persons.

Total Time

This recipe will take about 20 minutes to cook. Of which about 10 minutes will be dedicated towards cooking, and the rest will be required for preparation.

Ingredients

The various components of this dish requires individual amounts of ingredients to be made properly

Salmon:

- 2 x 150 gram Salmon Fillets With Skin On
- About 1 teaspoon of Olive Oil

Courgette:

- 2 Large sized straight courgettes
- 1 de-stoned and chopped ripe Avocado
- ½ of a finely chopped garlic clove
- A Small handful of Parsley
- A Small Handful of Cherry Tomatoes
- A Small Handful of Black Olives
- About 2 tablespoons of Toasted Pine Nuts

Nutritional Values

- Calories : 208
- Fat : 13g
- Saturated Fat : 3.1g
- Carbohydrates :0g
- Protein : 20g
- Sodium 59mg
- Dietary Fiber :0g
- Cholesterol : 55mg

How to Make The Dish

- o The first step which you will need to do is season the salmons, and to do that you are going to need to follow a very simple step of oiling and rubbing up the fishes with salt and Pepper

- Turn on your Air Fryer and put it at a temperature of 180 degree Celsius, put your prepared Salmon in your Cooking Dish and gently put it inside your Cooking Chamber. It should take around 10 minutes for your Salmon to become lovely and crisp with a fine texture.
- While the Salmon is being cooked, you can turn around tend to your Courgette. To prepare your Courgette, you are going to need to use a Spiralizer or Julienne Peeler on them. Once done, put it aside.
- For the sauce, take your avocado, parsley, garlic and some of the seasoning and put them in a mini chopper or food processor until they have been blended smoothly.
- Next, what you will need to do is chop up your tomatoes and olives, set them to one side and toss in the Courgette into the sauce.
- Divide them between two plates alongside the tomatoes, olives and top it off with salmon.
- Serve it with some pine nuts scattered all around.

Your Free Gift

- I wanted to show my appreciation that you support my work so I've put together a free gift for you.

EASY BONE BROTH: TOP 45 Recipes For Instant Weight Loss And Powerful Health Improvement.

http://www.iqtravels.com/gift-easy-bone-broth

- Just visit the link above to download it now.
- I know you will love this gift.
- Thanks!
- Richard Leroy

Conclusion

It has been a very long journey with you up until now, and I do hope that this book has been helpful in letting you know at least some new recipes which you thought were not possible to be done using Air Fryer. The concept of Air Fryer is still at a very early stage, but with the advent rising of more and more health conscious people, Air Fryer is slowly getting into the Main Stream market and is becoming one of the more prominent Kitchen Appliance for a Health Buff.

The recipes in this book are nothing but just the tip of the Ice Berg, and these were written to give you a glimpse of the true potential of your Air Fryer and what more can be done with it.

From this point on, I will encourage you to explore as much as possible, experiment with you own ingredients and make the next ground breaking masterpiece using your very own Air Fryer!

I thank you again for purchasing this book, and I hope that you had as much fun reading it as I had writing it.

Copyright 2016 by Richard Leroy - All rights reserved.

All rights Reserved. No part of this publication or the information in it may be quoted from or reproduced in any form by means such as printing, scanning, photocopying or otherwise without prior written permission of the copyright holder.

Disclaimer and Terms of Use: Effort has been made to ensure that the information in this book is accurate and complete, however, the author and the publisher do not warrant the accuracy of the information, text and graphics contained within the book due to the rapidly changing nature of science, research, known and unknown facts and internet. The Author and the publisher do not hold any responsibility for errors, omissions or contrary interpretation of the subject matter herein. This book is presented solely for motivational and informational purposes only.

Lightning Source UK Ltd.
Milton Keynes UK
UKOW06f1949030717
304605UK00008B/855/P